Seven Essential Daily Prayers

Build a Firewall Every Morning
For Your Spiritual Survival

Loren L. Fenton, D.Min.

A Product of GoodlifeNews! Productions
College Place, Washington, USA
https://goodlifenews.co

Cover Art Photo Credit: Can Stock Photo

ISBN: 978-1-7941122-6-1

Dedication

First: to the God of Heaven who both hears and answers the sincere heart-felt prayers of every soul at any time day or night. He is always there.

Second: To the sacred memory of my mother, Oral D. (Wilson) Fenton who taught me from my "cradle days" the value and joy of talking to Jesus about all the concerns of life, large or small.

Third: To the memory of Elder Glenn Coon, whose books and ministry in the "ABC Prayer Crusade" made a profound impact on my personal prayer life.

Fourth: To the innumerable "prayer warriors" I have known and admired in their passion for teaching Spirit-filled living to the family of God.

Contents

Acknowledgments

First: *There are not enough words to thank my wife Ruth, the love of my life, chief encourager, patient listener, wise counselor, and number one raving fan. What a lady! My joy in her is truly boundless.*

Second: *I am eternally grateful for the kind, patient teachers who guided my learning experience from early elementary school through high school, college, and grad school. Each one placed an indelible mark on my faith and understanding of language, philosophy, and how things work in this world.*

Third: *A special shout-out to Pastor Nathan Hellman for his invaluable counsel about the cover layout, graphics, and content. It didn't take much of his time, but his trained artistic eye spotted issues I would never have noticed. Thanks, Nate! May God bless you in your daily service for Him.*

Fourth: *Two beta/proof-readers who graciously lent their skills to review the raw self-edited manuscript. Sally Daley and Debbie Lynch-Christian, your independent observations and suggested revisions improved my original work by quantum leaps. ¡Muchas gracias, mis amigas!*

Introduction

Prayer has always been an important part of my life. As a young child, my mother taught me to "talk to Jesus" every night at bedtime. I grew up attending church, and early on I often led our church youth group in prayer. At home, our family paused to pray before every meal. My turn to "say grace" at the table happened regularly.

The idea of prayer was such an integral part of our lives that I didn't think very much about it. That changed when I was sixteen years old.

One evening, I had a hard time settling down for the night. I tossed and turned for an hour or more. Everyone else was already chasing dreamland fantasies, but not me. Our big old farmhouse was lighted only by faint moonlight seeping through the windows. Everything was quiet—except for the heavy breathing of my slumbering family. I thought a walk outside might help me relax.

I dressed and headed out the back door, walking along the lane that led to the fields of our farm. The night was beautiful, clear and cool, with a gentle, nearly imperceptible breeze.

Out under the open sky, I talked with God. Gazing at the brilliant heavens I opened my heart to the Lord.

"Jesus," I said, "tonight I accept you as my personal Savior and invite you to be Lord of my life. Right now, I open my heart's door to you. Please come into my heart and live in me!"

In all the years of my childhood and youth, never once had I taken this step. But, standing there alone on our dusty lane, under the Milky Way blazing in all its glory, that prayer became an anchoring milestone in my spiritual journey.

"Lord, what do you want me to do with my life?" I asked.

In that moment I heard God's voice calling me to tell other people about his amazing grace and forgiveness. I accepted, and the compass of my life was reset to highways and byways I never imagined.

Now, nearly six decades later, I look back with amazement. Those tiny first steps of faith began a lifetime walk with my Heavenly Friend.

I didn't know it as I walked that dusty lane, but— looking back—I can see God's hand at work, leading, guiding, and empowering my walk with Him—teaching me new lessons in prayer all along the way.

In early December 2011—after retiring earlier

that year—I signed a lease to use my Dodge Ram truck delivering fifth-wheel RVs and travel trailers to dealerships for their inventory.

I loved my new "owner-operator" status in this tiny niche of the trucking industry. The job involved long, exhausting days, traveling the highways of America and Canada. I reveled in the beauty of God's handiwork I saw through my windshield. My songs of praise blended with the engine's diesel growl in spontaneous concerts of joy.

Unfortunately, the devil was out there on the road with me, too. During those long driving hours, my mind sometimes wandered into unhealthy areas of imagination. I knew that indulging in impure thoughts would sow bitter seeds of tragic loss in my spiritual experience and could inevitably destroy everything I held dear. The fruit would be bitter, indeed. There's no way I wanted to go there!

I prayed for God's help. I spoke right out loud there in the cab of my truck, traveling sixty-miles-per-hour on the freeway with a 38' fifth-wheel trailer behind me.

"Lord," I said, "I want purity in my mind! I don't want these evil thoughts. I reject them. I need the purity that only you can give!"

To my amazement, the negative imaginations evaporated like morning mist disappearing in bright sunbeams. I was free.

Over the next several months my simple prayer expanded. I began adding "righteousness in my heart," and "integrity for my life" whenever another tempting thought would rear its ugly head. Each time, God graciously removed those errant, dark imaginations and replaced them with hope and peace.

As time passed, I began to sense God taking me on a new journey. Those basic three prayers—purity, righteousness, and integrity— were joined by four more: "joy for my spirit," "strength for my body," "wisdom for my counsel," and "to be a godly influence in the world."

Today, these seven "essential prayers" provide the basic blocks of a "firewall" I know I need for protection against daily attacks from the dark side. Of course, my prayers are never restricted to the seven only, but they are where I begin my day, every day. I cannot survive spiritually without making this vital connection with God.

Living in the ongoing progress of this journey is wonderful and exciting. I have presented my experience—and this message of the *Seven Essential Daily Prayers*—in live devotionals, numerous sermons, and an online course of recorded video lessons with PowerPoint presentations.

And, now this book.

My deepest prayer is for you to find a rich personal walk with God. I pray that you will experience a vibrant spiritual journey, an abiding hunger for purity and righteousness, and a daily infilling of God's *agápe* love.

May the thoughts I share in this small volume encourage you to that end.

Loren L. Fenton
College Place, Washington, USA
September 2019

Chapter One

Purity in My Mind

*That God's Agápe Love
May Live in My Heart Forever*

A carrier of light must never be a practitioner of darkness.

    Rome, Italy, c. A.D.66-67. An old man shivers as he sits alone, surrounded by cold stone walls in Rome's Mamertine Prison dungeon. This once-upon-a-time cistern—constructed six centuries earlier and located near the Forum—functions as a holding cell for political prisoners and mortal enemies of the Empire. Saul of Tarsus, as he is still known by Roman authorities, glances up at the large round hole in the ceiling above him. It's the only way in or out of this terrible place. He doesn't have much time left. Roman citizens convicted of sedition are usually beheaded in the public square. He hopes the next time he's lifted by ropes up through that hole he will be exonerated and freed, but he knows it could be his last exit from life itself.

The Apostle Paul's thoughts, however, are far from his current misery or his impending fate. Angels of God have visited him in the dungeon, warming his heart and bringing him an indescribable peace. He thinks of his young associate Timothy, working hard and doing his best to oversee the church at Ephesus, more than a thousand miles east of Rome.

One of the few privileges Paul did have is the freedom to write. Did he have a table and chair with writing materials, even in that awful hell hole? Did he dictate his message to a scribe? I'm not sure. But, one way or another he managed to get a letter composed and sent on its way to Timothy. It's a message of encouragement, promise, hope, and instruction.

Paul painted no rosy picture of the challenges Timothy faced in the task of proclaiming the gospel and leading the church in Ephesus. As a result of Paul's own previous ministry, thousands of people rioted for two whole hours in the Ephesian theater defending their goddess Diana, screaming "Great is Diana of the Ephesians!"[1]

Sitting in that Roman dungeon, Paul proclaimed with a prophetic pen: "Things are going to get a whole lot worse before they get better" (my own feeble paraphrase).

But Paul's vision is more than just for Ephesus. In that ancient prison, God opened the eyes of His faithful servant to future social conditions wherever and whenever believers worship the God of heaven.

---

[1] Acts 19:28, 34

There will be terrible times in the last days, Paul wrote. *People will be lovers of themselves, lovers of money, boastful, proud, abusive, disobedient to their parents, ungrateful, unholy, without love, unforgiving, slanderous, without self-control, brutal, not lovers of the good, treacherous, rash, conceited, lovers of pleasure rather than lovers of God, having a form of godliness but denying its power (2 Timothy 3:1-5).*

It doesn't take a Ph.D. to realize--we're there.

The good news in Paul's prophecy is that the "last days" means Jesus will very soon make another personal appearance on this planet! He's not coming this time as a helpless newborn baby in a first-century Bethlehem barn. Instead, he's coming as King of kings, and Lord of lords. All the angels of heaven come with him, shouting, blowing trumpets, opening graves. The risen saints of all ages spring forth with brand new, glorified bodies, claiming victory over death and the grave. They are joined by a vast throng of the living saved who blend their voices in joyous exclamations of hosannas and hallelujahs.

What a day that will be![2]

But, what does all this have to do with "Purity in My Mind," the first prayer in this list of *Seven Essential Daily Prayers?*

It all goes back to one of the Beatitudes Jesus stated in his Sermon on the Mount. With a crowd of fishermen, farmers, and other commoners pressed in close to catch his every word, he said, "Blessed are the

---

[2] See 1 Thessalonians 4:13-18

pure in heart, *for they shall see God".* (Matthew 5:8 emphasis mine).

To me, this promise means we will see him with our own living eyes, not just to "see" as in "understanding." The Apostle John, in the Book of Revelation, says, "Behold, he is coming with clouds, and every eye will see him, even they who pierced him" (Revelation 1:7). And, again, the angels who spoke to Jesus' disciples who were gazing into the sky where they last saw him, gave them this great assurance: "This same Jesus, who was taken up from you into heaven, will so come in like manner as you saw him go into heaven" (Acts 1:11).

The biblical evidence is clear. Every person in every corner of the planet will see and hear the arrival of King Jesus when he comes again. The proud and profane will see him, but in terror and panic they cry for the rocks and mountains to hide them from "the face of the Lamb" (Revelation 6:16). In stark contrast, those who are "pure in heart" are changed in an instant. Their old mortal bodies transform into immortality as they rush forward to greet their Jesus.[3]

I want to see Jesus like that! It is a major factor in my search for a victorious prayer life.

But, beyond my personal journey, I have a deep desire to be used by God to touch the lives of others with this same hope. This is the driving purpose of my life and ministry. I pray each person reading these pages will find the same inspiration I have found, and together we can meet Jesus face-to-face—in peace—when he comes

---

[3] See 1 Corinthians 15:51-56

again.

Believers with pure hearts will see God because they are filled with God's love. A pure heart empowers and produces *agápe* love—the kind of love God has for all Creation.

In the Apostle Paul's first letter to Timothy, he said, "The goal . . . is [*agápe*] love, which comes from a pure heart and a good conscience and a sincere faith" (1 Timothy 1:5).

Let's not miss Paul's message here. To rephrase just a bit, *the purpose of purity is to provide the soil where God's* agápe *love can grow.*

> **Key Concept:**
> *Moral purity is the catalyst for God's agápe love to thrive in our hearts.*

Agápe love is the heart of the gospel, the central theme of the entire Bible from Genesis to Revelation, the great motivating element in the heart of God yearning over his wayward children.

Agápe love was the nuclear core of Jesus' teaching, and the quality he most desired to see in his disciples. He said, "A new commandment I give to you, that you love [*agápe*] one another; as I have loved you, that you also love one another. By this all will know that you are my disciples, if you have [*agápe*] love for one another" (John 13:34, 35 NKJV).

But what, specifically, is *agápe* love? How is it different from any other kind of love? Why is it so important that we have this special kind of love ruling in our minds and hearts?

Let's find out.

In 336 B.C. at the age of 20, Alexander III of Macedon succeeded his father Phillip II as king. By the time Alexander the Great died a scant twelve years later—in 323 B.C—he had forged an empire so massive it extended from the eastern shores of the Adriatic Sea to the Indus River 3,200 miles to the east, and south to the upper reaches of the Nile in Southern Egypt. By 356 B.C. some 70 cities across that vast territory bore his name and were ruled by garrisons of Greek soldiers. Over the next two hundred years, Greek language and culture permeated every corner of the Empire, influencing everything from religious practices to entire social networks. Koiné Greek became a common language bridging the gap separating all the many diverse conquered nations.

The Greek language primarily recognized three different kinds of love.[4] They had different names for each. By the time the New Testament was written (using Koiné Greek) in the 1st century A.D., these three names for "love" were as commonly known and used as much as we might talk about the three forms of H_2O (solid, liquid, gas) today.

Here are the three Greek words for "love":

Eros—**physical (sensual, sexual) love.** From *eros,* we get our current English word "erotic." For the ancient Greeks—and New Testament authors—this did not carry the taboos or social stigmas that it often does today. It simply was a way to express the element of

---

[4] For the record, a fourth Greek word (*storge*) was used to indicate natural empathy/affection a parent would have toward a child.

physical arousal and attraction in human relationships.

***Philos*—Brotherly love; friendship.** The American city of Philadelphia, Pennsylvania was named to carry the identity "The City of Brotherly Love." *Philos* is the bonding love of friends, or soldiers in a tight-knit unit, or kids who have grown up together and maintain their connection well into adulthood because of loyalty, common experiences, and just because they still like to hang out with each other.

***Agápe*—Love as a principle; Godly love; unconditional; unbroken.** The best example of *agápe* is found in John 3:16, "For God so *loved* the world that he gave his one and only Son, that whoever believes in him shall not perish but have eternal life."

The devil hates *agápe* love!

In our age, he has brought out all the big guns in his arsenal to do everything in his power to demolish it. *Agápe* love is the heart of God and is the very first fruit of the Holy Spirit dwelling in a believer's heart.[5] In Satan's eyes *agápe* must be relentlessly attacked and destroyed. He knows by destroying God's love in our hearts he can break our bond with God and His gift of eternal life. The Apostle Peter warns, "Be self-controlled and alert. Your enemy the devil prowls around like a roaring lion looking for someone to devour" (1 Peter 5:8).

The evil foe of heaven knows *the most effective way to eliminate true, godly love in the human heart is to destroy purity.* For this reason, our first line of defense— the very first building block for constructing a daily firewall

---

[5] See Galatians 5:22

for spiritual survival—must be to pray for purity in our thought life.

Thoughts become imaginations, and if allowed to grow, imaginations become desires, desires become resolutions, resolutions become actions. If we act out those ungodly thoughts, we sin, and the devil's forces win the battle.

And, make no mistake, this battle is very, very real.

Our world today is a moral swampland. Social media, cable television, pop music, and magazines spew non-stop sleaze and hyper-sexed programming. Internet porn sites are visited more than Netflix, Amazon, and Twitter combined! A recent report stated that over 70% of the American population are porn consumers! It is impossible to avoid. Even the advertisements capitalize on the allure of illicit indulgence.

In truth, this rampant immorality is nothing new. It's been around since before Noah and the biblical Flood.

*The Lord saw how great man's wickedness on the earth had become, and that every inclination of his heart was only evil all the time." (*Genesis 6:5).

In the first century, James, the brother of Jesus wrote to the church, "Pure and undefiled religion before God and the Father is this: to visit orphans and widows in their trouble, and to keep oneself unspotted from the world" (James 1:27).

How in the name of the Lord are we supposed to do that while sitting in the middle of this swamp of evil?

Let's admit it. We've all drunk the swamp water.

Paul defines our situation clearly when he says, "All have sinned and come short of the glory of God" (Romans 3:23). A few verses earlier in the same chapter he quotes several Old Testament prophets from a thousand years earlier: "There is none righteous, not even one; there is none who understands, no one who seeks God. All have turned away, they have together become worthless; there is no one who does good, not even one" (Romans 3:10-12).[6]

The Prophet Isaiah agrees. He declares: "All our righteousnesses are as filthy rags" (Isaiah 64:6).

The bottom line of all this is: We can *never* win the quest for moral purity in this life in our own strength. Not by willpower. Not by determination. Not by force of personality. Not even by senility! Our only hope is in the power of the Holy Spirit filling us with his presence.

But that truly is good news, because survival is possible! God's amazing grace gives us hope.

"The wages of sin is death, but the gift of God is eternal life in Christ Jesus our Lord" (Romans 6:23). When we accept Jesus Christ as our personal Savior and Lord, we receive our new life in him. "Therefore, if anyone is in Christ, he is a new creation; the old has gone, the new has come!" (2 Corinthians 5:17).

That new life in Christ is, in fact, *eternal* life. It begins now, even before we get to heaven. When we are "in Christ," and Christ is "in us," we have Christ's righteousness and purity in our mind and heart. "Jesus was tempted an all points as we are, yet without sin"

---

[6] (See also Psalm 14:1-3; 53:1-3; Ecclesiastes 7:20)

13

(Hebrews 4:15). Therefore, it is "Christ in [us], [which gives us] the hope of glory" (Colossians 1:27b), even right now, today.

The big question for believers becomes, How do we maintain our new life in Christ? With temptations multiplied every day on every hand, how do we even get through an hour—let alone a whole day or a lifetime—with this new life intact?

Paul gives us the key: "We walk by faith and not by sight" (2 Corinthians 5:7 NKJV). Here are a few "living-the-life" principles from the Bible, written for our encouragement:

- "Let this mind be in you which was also in Christ Jesus" (Philippians 2:5 NKJV).

- "How can a young [person] keep his way pure? By living according to Your word" (Psalm 119:9).

- "Your word I have hidden in my heart, that I might not sin against you" (Psalm 119:11 NKJV).

So, even though spiritual purity is totally and completely a gift from God, the individual choices we make are crucial to successfully living for him.

Purity is a gift for which we can pray. Maintaining purity is a choice. God gives the victory. We live the victory by our choices.

Certain routines and habits contribute mightily to preserving the peace with God we receive in Christ.

Here is the key habit/routine I've found works best for me:

- *First*, set a specific time every morning to read

14

something from the Bible before you get into the busyness of the day.

There are many Bible-reading plans available. Using a plan you get from another source is fine, or you can design your own plan. You may decide to study a specific subject or focus on a special passage, or it may be as simple as beginning with Genesis 1:1 and reading straight through to Revelation 22:21. That's the plan I've personally followed most often since beginning my Christian journey at age sixteen. As I write this, I am now 74 and—with God's grace and blessing—I recently completed my 40th trip through the Word. I can only praise God for the blessings I have received in every reading. God is good!

- *Second*, spend some time in quiet contemplation—meditation—on the passage(s) you read.

- *Third*, memorize some scriptural promises. In this way you will internalize the power of God's Word, giving you strength for the day to resist and overcome the devil's temptations.

"Finally, brothers, whatever is noble, whatever is right, whatever is pure, whatever is lovely, whatever is admirable—if anything is excellent or praiseworthy—think about such things" (Philippians 4:8).

Remember: A heart of purity empowers godly, unconditional, unbroken *agápe* love. The enemy's goal is to break the bond of love between us, our fellowmen, and God.

By our freewill choice, we receive God's gift of

love, forgiveness, and moral power.

Chapter Two

Righteousness in My Heart

That I May be Filled with the Holy Spirit

Blessed are those who hunger and thirst for righteousness, for they will be filled. - Matthew 5:6

MOUNT EREMOS, GALILEE, ISRAEL, February 1997—I absolutely couldn't help myself. I blinked back tears, drinking in the scene around me. Not far away I noticed some pastors from our tour group also deeply emotional. Some silently wept with awesome wonder in that moment on the mountain.

Winter rains were over, at least on the day we visited. Fluffy white clouds drifted lazily across a bright blue sky, sailing east from the distant Mediterranean toward Jordan, Saudi Arabia, and Iraq. A springtime feel dominated everything. Birds sang. Early flowers were budding. The grounds of the Franciscan chapel—built near this traditional site of the Sermon on the Mount— were groomed to perfection. Just to the north, adjacent to the church property, a broad gentle valley sloped southward toward the valley floor.

The formation of the landscape could easily accommodate several thousand people sitting in nature's open-air theater. The acoustics were phenomenal. If everybody was quietly listening, a speaker at the bottom of the hill could be heard and understood by the entire crowd.

I thought of Jesus speaking to people in that very spot.

A vibrant, living green covered the surrounding hills. Below us, the Lake of Gennesaret (Sea of Galilee) stretched away to the south, emptying into the Jordan River on its journey to the Dead Sea.

I caught my breath.

The scene reminded me of my early years as a young farm boy growing up in Washington State's Yakima Valley. Those same-looking fluffy white clouds often drifted across our farm in springtime, dotting grey sagebrush hills to the north and south with great shadows moving across the landscape. The blue sky of Israel reminded me of azure summer skies above my head in childhood. The sparkling beauty of Galilee spoke to me of America's great Pacific Northwest.

Something deep inside me opened to a knowledge of God's love that day such as I had never encountered before.

For some strange reason I have yet to understand, the experience became an epiphany for me—a living encounter with the living God. Without spoken words, I heard my own inner voice responding to the beauty all around me.

Jesus knows me! He understands me! He grew up and lived in this place so like the valley of my own childhood. Yes, Jesus knows and understands me! And he loves me!

No words were adequate to describe my joy, only tears. The thrill has never ceased, even to this day.

I can well imagine Jesus looking south beyond the mountainside, past the blue Galilean waters, and perhaps glancing toward the rising hills to the east. Over there in a region known as Decapolis (aka "Ten Towns") small settlements of mostly Greek heritage dotted the shoreline. Non-Jews felt no restrictions to raising pigs. The area swarmed with herds numbering into the thousands.

On the day Jesus delivered his sermon on Mt. Eremos, was he thinking about the demoniacs in the region of Decapolis whom he would soon set free from their captivity?[7] I wonder if he—even then—heard their desperate cry for deliverance, their hearts hungering for righteousness and peace.

I wonder if perhaps Jesus also thought about the story he would share later—the one about the boy who left home with his inheritance, only to find himself herding pigs for a farmer "in a far country."[8] The region of Decapolis east of Galilee could have been the place.

---

[7] See Matthew 8.

[8] See Luke 15:11-32

The boy was just a restless farm kid hungry for excitement. Maybe late teens, early twenties.

You know the story. Kid gets bored with farm life, asks dad for his inheritance, gets it, and heads out to find a life of excitement. After blowing all his wealth on wine, women, and song he finds himself a long way from home, broke, abandoned, starving in a pigsty.

In a flash of brilliant insight, the kid realizes the stupidity of his situation, leaves the pigs, and hits the road. He's going home!

Dad sees him coming from a great distance away, drops everything and rushes—runs!—to embrace his boy. Tears flow. Party time! Celebrate! Kill the fatted calf! The boy is back!

We don't know all the details about this boy and his family, of course. The location of their farm, for instance. And, where—exactly—did the kid go when he left home for his grand adventure?

Jesus didn't say. But it's not hard to imagine some strong possibilities.

Consider this: Jesus grew up in Nazareth of Galilee. The rich soil and generally mild climate made farming and agriculture a mainstay of the area's economy.

Just to the north of Nazareth—about 5 miles away, or an hour's walk—sat the city of Sepphoris. Around the time of Jesus' birth, Herod Antipas began rebuilding Sepphoris as the capital city of Galilee.

The process took many years. As the city grew in importance and the population swelled, the needs for

SEVEN ESSENTIAL DAILY PRAYERS

builders, craftsmen, and a steady, reliable source of foodstuffs and other supplies increased by the day.

It is entirely possible that Joseph took his carpentry skills—and his young adopted son Jesus—to Sepphoris to help build the new capital city for their province. They could have commuted on the ten-mile round trip every day leading a donkey carrying their tools.

Could it be that on those trips to the city, or perhaps in the Sepphorian marketplace, the young Jesus met and become acquainted with two boys from a local farm family bringing their produce to sell? We don't know this, of course. It's all pure speculation. But for me—even though it's completely imaginary—it provides a wonderful backstory for Jesus' parable of the lost boy in Luke 15.

At the beginning of his ministry when Jesus gave the Sermon on the Mount, did he glance toward Decapolis on the eastern shore of the Sea of Galilee? Might he have thought about a friend from his youth, a friend whom he loved who chose to leave the warm security of home and hearth, looking for excitement in the pagan Greek cities of the Decapolis? I like to think so. Especially the part about the boy going home.

When the young prodigal son "came to himself," he realized all the exciting thrills money can buy cannot satisfy the heart. It wasn't just the emptiness of his stomach driving him to go home. It was the aching hunger of his spirit, borne from understanding his sins for what they were. He immediately determined to confess them to his father. And his father accepted him!

Love and grace won the day, with lavish gifts pouring from the father's heart. His robe. His ring. His own sandals for the barefoot boy. Strike up the band. It's time to sing and dance.

"This, my son," he cried, "was dead and is alive again; he was lost and is found! (Luke 15:32).

A precious story for Jesus' message to his audience on Mt. Eremos at the beginning of his ministry. Looking at the waiting crowd of farmers and fishermen, Jesus began to teach.

- *Blessed are the poor in spirit, for theirs is the kingdom of heaven.*

- *Blessed are those who mourn, for they will be comforted.*

- *Blessed are the meek, for they will inherit the earth.*

- *Blessed are those who hunger and thirst after righteousness, for they will be filled.*

- *Blessed are the merciful, for they will be shown mercy.*

- *Blessed are the pure in heart, for they will see God.*

- *Blessed are the peacemakers, for they will be called the sons of God.*

- *Blessed are those who are persecuted because of righteousness, for theirs is the kingdom of heaven* (Matthew 5:3-10).

Did you notice the awesome promise right in the middle of those eight beatitudes? "Blessed are those who hunger and thirst after righteousness, *for they will be filled!"* (Matthew 5:6, emphasis supplied).

I read those words now and realize how hungry I am. Not just hungry—I'm starving! I'm totally empty. My natural spiritual heart is weak and fainting. I can't even stand up on my own. If I don't get revived, I'll die for sure.

In chapter one, "Purity in My Mind," we saw what Paul wrote in his letter to the Romans: "There is none righteous, no, not one" (Romans 3:10).

> **Key Concept:**
> *Righteousness is a gift to the unrighteous from a Holy Father whose heart is filled with grace.*

So, there we are—*wretched, pitiful, poor, blind, and naked* (Revelation 3:17). Quite a picture, isn't it? And, sadly, oh so true.

Those words from Revelation also come directly from Jesus himself, not just to a ragged crowd of first-century followers assembled on a Galilean hillside, but to you and me, right now, today.

Back in Romans, we read, "The kingdom of God is not eating and drinking, but righteousness and peace and joy in the Holy Spirit" (Romans 14:17). A few verses later Paul adds, "Everything that was written in the past was written to teach us, so that through endurance and the encouragement of the Scriptures we might have hope" (Romans 15:4).

Hope! What a powerful word—especially when we're hungry! Jesus promises us in the fourth beatitude that people who hunger and thirst for righteousness will, indeed, be filled. His assurance truly gives us hope, even in our hopelessness.

Let's explore how this works.

Here are three keys which—for me—help unlock the door of God's storehouse filled with abundant grace for our aching needs:

Key #1; Recognize and Embrace the Source of Spiritual Hunger

When I was thirteen years old, I entered my freshman year of high school. Along with nearly all the other boys in our farming community, I enrolled in Vocational Agriculture and became a member of the Future Farmers of America (FFA). A major portion of the VoAg class was spent in shop activities, where we learned various practical skills needed for successful farming—things like welding, carpentry, machinery operation and repair, etc. The shop was well equipped with tools, workstations, and everything needed for us to learn the best practices for modern agriculture through hands-on experience.

One wall of the shop held a large panel displaying all the hand tools anyone would need for a project. Pliers, wrenches, various screwdrivers, hammers and such hung on the board, each with its own spot marked by a painted silhouette showing the outline of the tool. Our VoAg teacher, Mr. Chevy Chase, very strictly enforced a rule that every tool must be in its place when the bell rang at the end of class. We were supposed to return every tool we were using to the board, then we could be dismissed.

Mr. Chase's system worked exceptionally well in preserving the shop's supply of tools and equipment. One day, however, a small pair of pliers slipped into the leg pocket of my coveralls, walked with me right out the door, and found a new home on our farm. No one at school seemed to miss it. Not even Mr. Chase. I felt quite smug because I "got away with it."

Fast forward a couple of years to the night under the stars when I walked and talked with God, giving my life to Him, and heard Him calling me to a lifetime of Christian ministry.[9] Not long after that life-changing encounter with the Holy Spirit my father, my brother, and I were working on a project in our home-shop shed. My dad went looking for something in his toolbox and came across a pair of pliers he didn't recognize.

"What are these pliers?" he asked. "I never put them in here. Where'd they come from?"

I didn't say a word, but my brother glared at me with an accusing stare. He didn't tell Dad either, but later he confronted me.

"You stole those pliers from the Ag shop, didn't you!" His tone carried more accusation than a question.

I still wouldn't admit it, but he continued, "I know you did. I recognize those pliers from school. You stole them and brought them home!"

I didn't say anything, and the conversation was dropped. I honestly don't remember all the exact details of what happened next, but the pliers stayed in their new home. And, other than my brother, I don't think anyone

---

[9] See Introduction, pp. 1-3.

else ever knew. Except there was a little whispering voice in my head that popped up at the most unexpected times telling me, *Thief! You know you stole those pliers. You're as guilty as sin!*

Fast forward again. This time about six more years.

Life was good in the Spring of 1967. I was getting ready to graduate from college with my bachelor's degree in theology. The girl of my dreams—a newly minted Registered Nurse—had agreed to marry me(!), and we were getting excited as our big day in early June grew closer and closer. Immediately after my graduation in August, I would begin pastoral ministry in Portland, Oregon. We had a beautiful brand-new car that we both loved. We were young and alive with hopes and dreams for our future. We both had great jobs—and we both loved Jesus. I didn't think life could get any better. Love is grand!

One night we parked under the stars and talked about the life we were entering together, and about the Second Coming of Christ. The greatest event of all ages seemed so near. We both wanted to be ready for Jesus to come soon so we could live eternally with Him in the Earth made new. Our hearts beat as one that evening, swelling with love and hope.

Thief! You know you stole those pliers. You're as guilty as sin!

There was the pesky inner voice reminding me again of such a little transgression from years before. Why wouldn't it just go away!

The "voice" continued, *Not only that. You also*

lifted a can of pop from the grocery store that same year. What makes you think you're good enough to go to Heaven?

I took Ruth's hand in mine. "Sweetheart," I began, "There's something I need to tell you, and something I need to do. Years ago, when I was just starting high school, I stole a pair of pliers and a can of pop. I need to go home and make those things right."

The next day we looked at the calendar and chose an early upcoming date when we could visit my old home 100 miles to the west.

My parents were delighted to see us. Ruth stayed and visited with them while I drove into town. It was a weekday, so I knew school would be in session. I drove into the high school parking lot and found a spot near the VoAg shop and classroom. My heart pounded as I tried to walk calmly into the building.

Mr. Chase was still teaching the same classes all these years later. I saw him sitting at his desk as I entered the classroom and glanced through his office window. A quick knock on the open door brought an instant surprised grin of delight to his face.

"Loren Fenton? What a surprise! Come in and have a seat!" He motioned toward a chair across the desk from his. "What brings you here? It's good to see you!"

"Well," I began, "I came to bring you something."

I pulled a new pair of pliers from the bag in my hands and handed them to him.

"This is to replace some pliers I took out of the shop when I was here as a student. This has been weighing on my conscience for the last eight years, and I decided I'd better come and make it right."

He shook his head in disbelief.

"Really? That's hard to believe! I never would have suspected you. But I appreciate you coming. It's encouraging when these things happen."

"I'm sure you've probably had others come with similar confessions," I said.

"Yes, I have," he answered. "But not after eight years!"

The folks at the grocery store were equally as gracious. A great weight left my spirit as I completed both purposes of this journey.

It wasn't the value of the items. It was knowing I had done the right thing making restitution for a couple of stupid actions from my youth. The condemning voice in my head was silenced forever about a stolen pair of pliers and a can of pop. I was free!

I learned a great truth through the experience of confession and restoration: (A) Sin creates "Spiritual Anxiety," aka "guilt." (B) This Holy Spirit-inspired *guilt* convicts me of my *wrongness*, which (C) Creates *remorse*, and (D) Leads to *repentance* and *restitution*.

Owning the guilt is the first step toward receiving the fullness of God's promises and power to live a life of righteousness.

Key #2; Personally Accept (by faith) Christ's Righteousness as Your Own

I relate the above story, not to say or imply those two little incidents from my early high school experience are the worst things I ever did or infer that we gain God's forgiveness by our works of repentance. Far from it!

Sadly, I've had to own and confess other *big* sins more times than I can count. It breaks my heart that I still wander from God. I still need to seek His forgiveness and grace every day I live and breathe.

It's encouraging to know I'm not alone.

The Apostle Paul exclaims in Romans, "What a wretched man I am! Who will rescue me from this body of death?" (Romans 7:24). Paul doesn't stop there, however. He immediately answers his own question, "Thanks be to God through Jesus Christ our Lord!" (Romans 7:25).

The central theme of Paul's ministry was that *the only hope for sinners is the righteousness of Christ.* As we put our faith and trust in Him, he exchanges His own righteousness for our filthy rags of sin.

"God made him (Christ) who had no sin to be sin for us, so that in him we might become the righteousness of God" (2 Corinthians 5:21).

Jesus said, "For God so loved the world that he gave his one and only Son, that whoever believes in him shall not perish but have eternal life" (John 3:16).

Such a simple truth. Righteousness comes to us not by our personal efforts, but as a gift from a loving God who cares for each of us personally.

All we have to do is accept His gift with thanksgiving and praise. As we trust His promise, He fulfills His promise, "Blessed are those who hunger and thirst for righteousness, for they will be filled" (Matthew 5:6).

Thus, the second essential daily prayer—the second building block for our spiritual firewall—is for "righteousness in my heart." God's gift is always ready any time day or night whenever we're "hungry" for him.

Are you hungry? What are you waiting for? Right now is a great time to open your heart to Jesus. He knows your every need. He has a bountiful supply of hope and healing for you.

Just ask.

Key #3; Choose Every Day to Live God's Love

God's promises are sure, but we have choices to make every day. Two roads are constantly open before us. One is the road of peace with God. The other is the road of self-serving disobedience.

On our own, we are helpless and doomed to failure, but choosing to be filled every day with God's love we can move forward to live for him with integrity.

Let's explore that in Chapter Three, "Integrity in My Life."

Chapter Three

Integrity in My Life

That My Witness for God will be Uncompromised

"The most important persuasion tool you have in your entire arsenal is integrity." — Zig Ziglar

"'You are my witnesses,' declares the Lord, 'and my servant whom I have chosen'" (Isaiah 42:10).

Well, you know from the last chapter I stole some stuff when I was a kid in high school. It obviously wasn't any big deal by human standards—just a pair of pliers and a can of pop—the pettiest of petty larceny. Certainly not up there with robbing a bank or grand theft auto or something else really serious. Even so, stealing is stealing, and that made me a thief—a breaker of the Eighth Commandment in God's Big Ten: "You shall not steal" (Exodus 20:15).

What relief I felt when I heard my teacher, Mr. Chase say, "You're forgiven!"

I also sensed God's forgiveness when I accepted the gift of Christ's righteousness to replace my guilt. Being a thief in the presence of Jesus doesn't have to be a bad thing. It depends entirely on the choices we make.

Two thieves were crucified with Jesus on Calvary. One refused to seek mercy and forgiveness, the other found salvation.[10] A sinner's guilt switched crosses on Golgotha, the "Place of the Skull." One man died in his own sin, a second died in the sin of another, a third man died forgiven, redeemed, and righteous in the sight of Heaven.

The third man's choice resulted in eternal salvation. There on the cross, he found freedom in Christ.

Sadly, I must admit that I'm not only a thief, I'm also a liar. No, I never lied on the witness stand in court, or told a fib to escape punishment.

But, then, there's this . . .

OUTLOOK GRADE SCHOOL, MRS. DAVENPORT'S 1ST GRADE CLASSROOM, 1951-1952. Imagine a bunch of lively first graders—I think there were around 30 of us. I still remember my friends. Tony, Paul, Robert, Linda, Leon, Judy, Billy, and many more. Our teacher, Mrs. Davenport, was a motherly soul who loved each of us. She even gave us all little gifts on her own birthday! We spent our days with "Dick and Jane" readers, learning numbers, playing outside at recess, and otherwise just being kids.

I was a social child, so I enjoyed all the time with other children my age. Every day was filled with busy

---

[10] See Luke 23:39-43

activities. After lunch, we got our own mats out of a storage closet and lay on the floor for naps. We all loved school—and Mrs. Davenport. First grade was fun.

Since six-year-olds often like to tell about their family life experiences, Mrs. Davenport provided a weekly time for us to share "news" from home. My classmates reported things like getting a new model airplane for their birthday, going on a vacation trip, or some other wonderful detail. Even things like Mom was going to have a new baby, or the dog had puppies last night. We were free to say whatever we wanted to say.

Except, I didn't have anything to report. Especially not anything unique or exciting. But I raised my hand anyway. Mrs. Davenport saw me and gave me a turn.

I rose slowly from my chair and stood with slumped shoulders, head bowed, eyes looking at the floor. I pretended to sniffle, and said in a weepy voice, "M-my Daddy d-d-died last night!"

To this day I have no idea where that little nugget of "fake" news came from or how it spread so rapidly through our farming community. Wildfire in a wheat field driven by a 30 mile-per-hour gale couldn't have gone any faster. Within minutes the phone at our house began ringing, ringing, ringing! Neighbors calling to deliver condolences and messages of support and sympathy to my mother.

"Oh, Mrs. Fenton, I'm so sorry to hear about your husband! If there's anything I can do, just call me."

Obviously, my mother was quite curious as to the source of this strange rumor about her husband.

"Well," she said, "I'm happy to tell you the report isn't true. Claude is sitting here in the kitchen, quite alive and well. Thank you for calling, but tell me, where did you get this story?"

Then, one-by-one she began to back-trace the gossip line until she learned that her youngest child had spun this wild tale in school during first grade "sharing time."

When I got home there was a loving confrontation during supper. Along with appropriate corrective measures (I'll leave that to your imagination), I was admonished with a verse from Scripture I never forgot: "Lying lips are an abomination to the Lord" (Proverbs 12:22a KJV).

Which brings me rather conveniently to the focus of this chapter, "Integrity in My Life."

I've found three main components to integrity: (1) Foundational honesty; (2) Dependability, and (3) Faithfulness.

Foundational Honesty

Through the years I've had fun swapping stories about lessons learned in childhood with John, one of my long-time friends. John's family were not church people, and he did not become a Christian until his mid-teens while he was away from home at a Christian boarding school. As often happens, after he gave his heart to Jesus his conscience became awakened to incidents of his life which he knew had to be confessed and repaired. One of those meant telling his father about something that had happened repeatedly over the course of several years during his earlier childhood.

I'll let John tell his story:

"Well, here's what happened. As a young kid, I had a love for sweets like you wouldn't believe. Candy, gum, cookies—whatever had sugar in it called my name! I could finish off a six-stick pack of Juicy Fruit gum in about an hour. I guess you could say I was pretty addicted. My "sweet tooth" was strong, alive, and well. I had no idea it wasn't good for me. If I had known, I wouldn't have cared though. If it was sweet, it was good, and I loved it.

"The problem was if I wanted to get candy from the store, I needed money, but I didn't have any. Even so, I knew where I could get some—my dad had a few coins in his dresser. Sometimes he and some friends got together for a game of poker. Their gambling didn't amount to any high stakes—just some loose pocket change to make their game more interesting. Dad kept his "gambling money" in a small box in one of the bedroom dresser drawers. I figured he wouldn't miss the few cents here and there that I needed for my candy fix. And I was right. He never suspected a thing.

I helped myself quite often to Dad's "bank" of easily available cash.

"When I was about 16 or 17, I was away from home at a Christian high school. The atmosphere there was very spiritual compared to my earlier home life. It wasn't that my parents weren't good people, they just weren't spiritual or religious in any way. The administrators, faculty, and staff at this school were different. Through their influence, I met the Lord and decided to live my life for him. That was a life-changing milestone.

"Very soon after my conversion, those 'candy coins' began to haunt me. I knew—among other things—I had to tell my dad about what I had done. It wasn't easy, but at the next home leave, I approached Dad and confessed to the error of my ways. I was thankful his response was quite measured and thoughtful.

"At the end of our conversation, I attempted to summarize my feelings.

"'Well,' I said, 'I guess honesty is always the best policy.'

"Dad's piercing black eyes drilled me like a laser beam. I knew something intense and important was about to happen. His voice sounded more serious than I had ever heard him speak before.

'Son,' he said, 'honesty is the ONLY policy.'"

Suffice it to say, my friend John never forgot the life lesson of the moment. It is still as fresh for him now, decades after the incident, as it was the day it happened. Some things we never forget!

What an important principle to live by—especially for Christians who claim to represent the God of heaven! The Ninth Commandment says, "You shall not bear false witness against your neighbor" (Exodus 20:16 NKJV).

I have encountered people who are so in the habit of lying they will lie when the truth would be better for their cause. The first lie recorded in the Bible is the serpent's statement to Eve in the Garden of Eden, "You will not surely die" (Genesis 3:4). Jesus called him (the devil) "the father of lies" (John 8:44).

And, just to be totally clear, there will be no liars in heaven. Describing God's heavenly city New Jerusalem, John the Revelator writes, "Nothing impure will ever enter it, nor will anyone who does what is shameful or deceitful, but only those whose names are written in the Lamb's book of life" (Revelation 21:27).

If we expect to live with integrity and total honesty there and then, we need to live by those same principles here and now. This life is the practice run for heaven.

Integrity is the natural fruit of an impeccable character.

Character is revealed in every daily life transaction we have with the people we encounter along life's pathway. As the Holy Spirit directs our words and actions, our business dealings will be strictly honest. "The Lord abhors dishonest scales, but accurate weights are his delight" (Proverbs 11:1).

The Lord delights in you and in your choices to deal truthfully and honestly in all aspects of your life.

Foundational honesty means living with transparency—what you see is what you get. It means we must not play games using tactics like hidden agendas, one-upmanship tricks, or deliberate attempts to confuse people for the purpose of control.

It also means we must discipline our thinking for

intellectual honesty.

> **Key Concept:**
> *Personal integrity confirms the authenticity of our words and actions.*

Emotions are good. They are given to us by our great Creator. Emotions drive the passion for our goals and intentions. Without them, we would get nowhere. But, good decisions (aka "choices") are not made on the basis of emotions alone. That is "emotionalism."

A healthier approach to decision making is combining our emotional drive with objective thinking. Objectively looking at all issues relative to whatever decision we're making will keep us balanced and result in stronger choices honoring God in everything.[11]

Dependability

Ruth and I have moved quite a few times during our life together, especially through the years of active ministry. Most of those moves were to distant cities or places where we knew few people. It was always quite a long process getting established in a new location. Besides finding a place to live, there was the matter of getting acquainted with the area. Where are the stores and shopping places? Which roads end in a dead-end? What is the best way to get from here to there? What grocery stores carry the nicest produce and have the best prices? Who is the most reliable auto mechanic?

That last question is no small item. Who can you

---

[11] See 1 Corinthians 10:31

trust? What shop will do the job right, but still not charge an exorbitant price for parts and labor? I don't begrudge someone a fair wage. Even Jesus taught that the worker deserves his wages (Luke 10:7), and Moses in his parting instructions to ancient Israel said, "Do not muzzle an ox while it is treading out the grain" (Deuteronomy 25:4). Both teach the same principle. No, I don't mind paying a good auto mechanic well, but there are two things I want to know.

First, can I depend on him (or her) for fairness and complete honesty in assessing the repairs or service my vehicle needs? In other words, does this person have a sterling character? Is he someone who always keeps his promises and is completely transparent with costs and projections? It is important to know these things!

Second, can I trust that the work done in this shop will be done right? I want to know for sure that when I drive out onto the road that I won't have a break-down or accident due to faulty workmanship. I want to know the worker is truly competent before they put a wrench to my car.

Dependability is the second component of integrity. Dependability is the product of Character and Competence.

Both are necessary.

When I'm teaching on this subject I often ask the audience, "Would you prefer a mechanic who is a really nice guy with an honest heart yet lacks competence, or would you want a highly skilled technician who might tell that you need a lot of repairs on your vehicle which are actually unnecessary?

The answer, of course, is neither. We need people who are both competent and have impeccable characters.

Character means that your word is your bond. People can believe what you tell them without fail.

Competence results from initial hands-on preparation followed by continuing education.

These two factors hold true regardless of your field of study or area of expertise. You can apply them to your life right now whatever your occupation or vocation. Proverbs 22:29 says, "Do you see a man who excels in his work? He will stand before kings."

To strive for excellence enhances dependability and upholds integrity.

Faithfulness

The third face of integrity is faithfulness.

Joseph did not endure the pit, Potiphar's house, and prison, because he knew he would end up in Pharaoh's palace. He simply remained faithful wherever he found himself. God did the rest.[12]

When my fiancée and I stood before our friend and minister on June 8, 1967, he asked both of us individually if we would be faithful to each other "so long as you both shall live." We both promised, "I will." By the grace of God, our vows have remained intact for over five decades! We can categorically say: Faithfulness has its

---

[12] Attributed to H. B. Charles, Jr. (To read the story of Joseph, see Genesis 39ff.)

rewards!

Our love has grown richer, stronger, deeper with every passing year. Every year brings new dimensions to our relationship we could never have imagined before. Our happiness and contentment continue to grow ever more beautiful. I'm not exaggerating. Just ask her!

Faithfulness is the key.

Faithfulness encompasses respect, devotion, patience, kindness, thoughtfulness, and courtesy. They all play a part, and they all pay rich dividends. "Be faithful, even to the point of death, and I will give you the crown of life" is a promise from Jesus to the church in Smyrna (Revelation 2:10). That promise is as valid and reliable for you and me today, just as it was for believers living in the 1st century A.D.

But, to what or to whom are we to be faithful? The answer is two-fold, and is found in Jesus' response to a question asked of him, "Which is the greatest commandment in the law?"

Jesus replied, "'Love the Lord your God with all your heart and with all your soul and with all your mind.' This is the first and greatest commandment. And the second is like it: 'Love your neighbor as yourself'" (Matthew 22:36-39).

There you have it.

Love God supremely, and your neighbor as yourself. If you love someone you will be faithful. It all stems from love—that is *agápe* love. Unconditional, unbroken, love as a principle. Love as a choice.

I have often been asked to tell a story to the

children in a worship service. Several times I have taken a bill out of my wallet and showing it to the kids I'll ask, "I want to give this money to God. How can I do that?"

Then I'll toss the bill into the air, saying, "If God is up in heaven, do you think I can just throw it up there so he can have it? How many of you think that would work?"

Of course, everybody can see how silly that is— even the adults who are listening in on this conversation!

No hands go up.

"Well," I'll say, "if that won't work, how can I get this money to God so he can use it?"

We ponder that for a few moments. Then I offer a suggestion.

"I know," I say. "Jesus told us, 'Whatever you [do] for one of the least of these brothers of mine, you did [to] me' (Matthew 25:40). So, that sounds to me that if we want to give this money to God, we can do that by doing something nice for someone in need. Maybe buying a sandwich for someone who is hungry or giving a warm coat to a person who is cold. What do you think? Does that sound like a good way to give this money to God?"

All the children nod in understanding. Their eyes shine with excitement as they head back to rejoin their family.

The only way to serve God, i.e. "be faithful to him," is to serve the needs of people around us. We need to learn to see the needs and learn the skills of appropriate responses. A great example is Jesus' story of the Good Samaritan.[13]

Perhaps we need to study this parable more deeply so we can absorb its focus and principles into our daily relationships with the people of our time.

A few years ago, I got the idea I would like to have a personal motto for my life. You probably have seen those clan mottoes displayed prominently on European family crests from the Middle Ages. That was the kind of short, pithy statement I wanted—not so much for my family as for myself. Something concise, powerful, and easily remembered. A catchphrase to live by.

I found a few examples I liked, but which were not exactly what I was looking for.

A Deo et rege - "For God and King."

Dant vires gloriam - "Strength gives glory."

Facta non verba - "Deeds not words."

I finally decided I would just have to write my own. Anyway, I thought, the exercise itself would make it more authentic.

I'm enough of a traditionalist I knew I wanted my motto to be in Latin—even though I had completely failed Latin class in high school! I did absorb enough of the language, however, to know some basic words and grammar. Writing this simple motto shouldn't be too hard.

Hmmmmm . . . .

It wasn't the language issue that pulled me up short. I suddenly came face to face with several questions about my life.

---

[13] See Luke 10:25-37

Who am I, really?

What am I about?

How do I want to live?

What is my life's purpose?

I had to stop and seriously think through the answers to these and other similar questions.

The exercise of writing this motto was like imagining what you would like to have engraved as an epitaph on your grave marker. What short statement would you like for summarizing your entire life and have it engraved in stone for anyone and everyone to read forever after you are gone?

After several years and several attempts, I finally arrived at my permanent motto. Here it is:

Vivere cum integritas in gracia Dei! "To live with integrity by the grace of God."

Yes, I'd like to have that motto carved into the marker of my final earthly resting place. I pray for strength to live that motto every day until I die. Without integrity, nothing else matters. Without God's grace, integrity fails.

We can only live with integrity as God gives us the power. Without Christ living in us via the presence of the Holy Spirit, our sinful, carnal nature consistently betrays our best intentions. Only as we are "in Christ" can our witness for him be uncompromised by our daily words and actions.

Will you join me in praying each day for the power to live a life of integrity? I'm praying that you will.

Chapter Four

Joy in My Spirit

That I May Face Each Day with Strength

The joy of the Lord is your strength![14]

Retirement centers—aka "rest homes," "senior care facilities" (and other euphemistic labels used for such places)—are not necessarily the happiest places on earth. Many, if not most of the residents suffer aches and pains common to advancing age. They often struggle with dimming eyesight, loss of hearing, fading strength, and/or other devastating health challenges. Sometimes—but not always—care staff are short-handed and overworked. Delayed attention to pressing needs can be terribly frustrating for an old person dealing with serious pain—or in a panic to use the bathroom! It's no wonder that "happy warriors" are few and far between in many of these

---

[14] Read the wonderful account which gave rise to this expression of celebration in Nehemiah 8.

facilities.

But then, there was Clarissa Archer.[15]

Clarissa always had a beautiful smile on her face. She simply glowed with peace and happiness. She had not escaped the difficulties and trials coming from 80+ years of life. Nevertheless, Clarissa was like a bright ray of sunshine everywhere she showed up.

That wasn't always the case. At times in the past, she grumbled and complained loudly about her old-age infirmities and inconveniences. She didn't like being old, and she didn't mind letting everyone around her know it. The "golden years" were *not* good, and she wasn't shy complaining about the way things were.

But then, one day Clarissa changed her attitude and became the cheerful person everyone loved.

Clarissa's son often came to take his mother into town for shopping and a sit-down restaurant meal. On this day he parked near the front door as usual and helped her into the car. After she was buckled in, Clarissa waited for her son to walk to the other side of the car and get into the driver's seat. In those few moments, she pulled the sun visor down to see the mirror on the backside. She sat gazing at her reflection as her son fastened his seatbelt and started the engine. A look of genuine concern crossed her face.

---

[15] "Clarissa Archer" is not her real name. However, this story is based on a true account of a very real lady living in a very real situation. I was her pastor for several years.

"I don't look happy," she said. "Christians are supposed to be happy. I'm going to practice being happy!"

It was more of a proclamation than a statement. Her voice carried the determination of a person making a much-needed and long-contemplated life adjustment. There was no mistaking her resolve. She was totally serious.

And she stuck to it!

That day marked the beginning of the last chapter in this precious lady's earthly life. From then on, Clarissa could not be seen without a smile on her face. Even now, many years after her death, the people who knew her still remember her as "the lady who was always smiling, always happy."

What an incredible testimony!

What was Clarissa's secret? She *chose* to be happy. Clarissa discovered happiness is a choice we make regardless of the circumstances in our life. Simply put, most people can choose to be happy, even in the middle of a miserable mess.

Under normal circumstances—even unpleasant

IMPORTANT: There is a genuine medical condition called "clinical depression." This may result from a variety of causes such as tumors, a chemical imbalance, or something else. Clinical depression cannot be "fixed" by just "choosing" to be happy. It is a serious issue which needs diagnosis and treatment by a qualified medical practitioner. If you think you or someone you know may be suffering from clinical depression, help is available. Don't neglect it. Talk to your doctor ones—we have a freewill choice. We can choose to be happy. Or, we can choose to be angry, upset, resentful, bitter, or any number of similar negative emotions.

A long time ago I went through an extremely difficult experience in my ministerial career. One night, without any advance warning, and while I was present—even "chairing" a church board meeting—the members present voted unanimously to remove me from office and, effective immediately, request a replacement pastor from our denominational headquarters. To say I was devastated would be a major understatement!

I went home after the meeting shocked, confused, and bewildered. What seemed like a million questions swirled through my mind like some kind of bizarre tornado descending from a clear, blue sky. *What just happened? What's going to happen next? What about my family? How am I going to support them? What will my wife and children think? Was I ever really called to ministry? Was my pastoral service really so bad? Why? Why? Why?*

I was hurt and angry. But, in my heart, I knew I had to put the needs of the church first. The church needed healing, and I knew for sure I was not the person who could bring it. With a heavy heart, I called my ministerial director.

I explained what had happened, then I heard myself saying words I never dreamed I would ever say.

"This congregation is badly damaged. For some reason I'm not sure I even understand, my presence here is causing more unrest and division. It's not getting better at all. In fact, it gets worse with every passing week. The best thing for this church is for me to resign so you can bring another pastor in who can be a healer."

The next morning at about 9:30 a.m. my phone rang. It was the Conference president.

"How long does it take you to drive to the office?" he asked.

"About three and a half hours," I answered.

"Good," he said. "I'll see you in here at one o'clock this afternoon."

The trip to headquarters was uneventful. My wife and I arrived promptly at the appointed time. The visit was cordial, but final. An hour later I was out of a job. I did not return to pastoral ministry for nearly three years.

The immediate aftermath of this disaster brought a flurry of transition events—moving to a different house, making major decisions for our family, getting our various affairs in order for whatever lay ahead. Every day brought new unforeseen challenges.

In the middle of all the frenzy, I remember intentionally making a bedrock decision.

I choose to forgive! I told myself in an internal conversation. *Bitterness is a poison that a person drinks hoping his enemy will die. I will not go down that road. I will not allow this experience to destroy me, my family, or my ministry. I have no idea what the future holds just now, but I will go there free from anger or resentment. I forgive those who caused this to happen. I forgive. I choose to be happy.*

A choice. The right choice.

From that moment until the very day as I write these words, I have seen God's hand leading me in countless uncharted paths of blessing. I can truly say with King David, "You have turned my mourning into dancing; you have put off my sackcloth and clothed me with gladness" (Psalm 30:11 NKJV).

There are times when I think I actually need to thank those who moved against me that dark night. Without their action, I would have missed an abundance of blessings I have received since then.

To be completely transparent, however, I must also confess, periodically I have to revisit my original choice to forgive. The Lord gives me ample opportunities to reaffirm my commitment to full forgiveness and its subsequent children, happiness and joy. Satan would love to recapture the hurt and grow the fruit of bitterness in my spirit. By God's continuing grace, I cannot—will not—yield to that temptation.

Many years ago, I came to realize regardless of how many or how bad negative events might be which unfold around you, if you turn them over to God he can, and does, redeem them for good.

"Rejoice in the Lord always. I will say it again: Rejoice! (Philippians 4:4).

So, mark this down: *When we choose happiness, God gives us joy.*

Joy is a gift from God. He sends it with the Holy Spirit taking up residence in the believer's heart.

"The fruit of the Spirit is love, joy, peace, patience, kindness, goodness, faithfulness, gentleness, and self-control. Against such things there is no law" (Galatians 5:22, 23).

The Holy Spirit's presence is a gift directly from Jesus to believers everywhere. He promised his disciples, "The Counselor, the Holy Spirit, whom the Father will send in my name, will teach you all things and will remind you of everything I have said to you" (John14:26).

Choosing happiness in the face of hardship, persecution, or misfortune is choosing to follow the whisperings of the Holy Spirit in your mind.

> **Key Concept:**
> *When we choose happiness and forgiveness, God blesses us joy.*

I'm not saying we should pretend that bad things and bad experiences don't exist. They obviously do, and no one enjoys them, but we don't need to be mentally and spiritually destroyed by evil events. We can choose to overcome. We can choose to survive. We can choose forgiveness and personal happiness. The choice is always ours.

Even so, we never lose the freedom to choose the other way if we decide we want to go in that direction.

Remember the story Jesus told about the boy who left home for adventure and finally came to his senses in a pig pen?[16] When he arrived back home everybody exploded into a great celebration. Dad was ecstatic. The servants killed the fatted calf. The band

---

[16] See Luke 15:11ff. Also, Chapter 2, "Righteousness in My Heart" in this book.

played. The whole family danced and partied into the night. The lost boy was home! Joy reigned in everybody's heart!

Everyone, that is, except the kid's big brother. When he found out what was going on, he blew up and refused to even go inside. His dad came out to try reasoning with his older son, but he would have none of it.

"Look!" he snapped, "All these years I've been slaving for you and never disobeyed your orders. Yet you never gave me even a young goat so I could celebrate with my friends. But when this son of yours who has squandered your property with prostitutes comes home, you kill the fatted calf for him!"

"My son," the father said, "you are always with me, and everything I have is yours. But we had to celebrate and be glad, because this brother of yours was dead and is alive again; he was lost and is found" (Luke 15:29-32).

Talk about a wet blanket! The kid's big brother couldn't have joy because he chose anger over happiness. His sour attitude had to have brought acute pain to his father's heart. One of his sons was lost, but alive—a cause for great rejoicing. The other cared for nothing but himself. I wonder if he saw his father's shoulders slump, or if he noticed the older man's slower, staggering steps as he turned back to the party in the house.

It is worth noting, in Luke 15 the only person without joy is the older brother. Everyone else is celebrating something lost but found. A coin. A sheep. A son. The only one who doesn't celebrate in these stories is this self-centered grown-up man-child who chooses hurt feelings over forgiveness, resentment over reason. He could have chosen love for his brother. He chose hatred instead. The fruit was hurt and heartache. The party lights shined a little dimmer for the grand occasion.

But this is what happens when we don't choose happiness. It not only blocks our own joy it also steals the wind from the wings of family and friends.

Near the end of the 5th century B.C. many Jews were allowed to return to Jerusalem from exile in Babylon. The city lay in ruins from the attacks of Nebuchadnezzar's army 70 years earlier. The protective wall was destroyed. All that remained were heaps of rubble scattered chaotically around the once-thriving center of Israel's glory days. The splendor of Solomon's once-upon-a-time magnificent empire had been reduced to dust and ashes by Babylonian soldiers. Centuries of Israel's and Judah's feckless kings and faithless priests bore the fruit of neglected holiness. The scene of ruined walls and burned-out buildings were enough to make even the stoutest heart tremble.

Political winds had shifted dramatically in the seventy years of exile. The Babylonians had fallen to the power of the Medes and Persians. The Persian King Artaxerxes I now sat on the throne of the new empire. History indicates that Artaxerxes I ruled with a tolerant hand, allowing for conquered peoples to retain and practice their own religions and customs. He was sympathetic to the needs of the Jews, permitting them to return to their homeland, and even authorizing the rebuilding of Jerusalem and its surrounding wall.

Artaxerxes I appointed his personal cupbearer, a Jew named Nehemiah as governor of Jerusalem. Nehemiah and a priest named Ezra led the overwhelming task of reestablishing the city and reconstructing the wall.

Beyond the physical structures, they also had to lay the philosophical and religious foundations for an entirely new populace. At least two, maybe three generations had come and gone during the seven decades of exile. The vast majority of the returned exiles had never seen their ancestral homeland. Living as a "chosen people" representing the Living God was strangely unfamiliar to them. They knew little or nothing of the culture, rituals, or fundamentals of their own Jewish religion. Growing up under the influence of pagan Persian beliefs and practices, they needed a comprehensive crash course in how they were supposed to live, the temple services, and what it all meant for them as individuals and as a distinct people.

A day was set for a great assembly. A speaking platform was built for the occasion. In the morning of the appointed day, Ezra the priest stood on the platform and read to the people all the words of the Law of Moses— what we now call the "Pentateuch," the first five books of our Bible: Genesis, Exodus, Leviticus, Numbers, and Deuteronomy. It took a long time to read it all. And it was heavy stuff. When the people heard what Ezra was reading, they broke down and wept.

> *And Nehemiah, who was the governor, Ezra the priest and scribe, and the Levites who taught the people said to all the people, "This day is holy to the Lord*

your God; do not mourn nor weep." For all the people wept, when they heard the words of the Law.

Then he said to them, "Go your way, eat the fat, drink the sweet, and send portions to those for whom nothing is prepared.; for this day is holy to our Lord. Do not sorrow, for the joy of the Lord is your strength" (Nehemiah 8:9, 10 NKJV).

The joy of the Lord is your strength!

Notice this: it is the "*joy of the Lord*" that gives you strength. In other words, it is the *joy in the Lord's heart*—because of his love for you—which becomes *your* strength when his Spirit lives in you.

"The kingdom of God is . . . righteousness, peace, and joy in the Holy Spirit" (Romans 14:17).

"Rejoice in the Lord always. I will say it again: Rejoice! (Philippians 4:4).

To summarize this chapter on our fourth essential daily prayer, here are a few suggestions for keeping your heart open and growing in the "joy of the Lord:"

1. Practice (choose) an attitude of gratitude!

2. Choose happiness. Choose to forgive anyone who has wronged you. Reject the temptation to indulge in a victimhood mentality.

3. Look for things to celebrate, like beauty in nature, gracious acts of kindness by other people, Bible

promises, or the gifts of life, health, and understanding.

4. Focus on the positive things of life. Set a time every day for personal Bible reading, memorization, reflection, and meditation. Accentuate the positive. Eliminate the negative.

5. There is power in praise! Psalm 22:3 says, "[God is] enthroned in the praises of Israel (NKJV). The KJV actually says that God *dwells* in our praise. What this teaches me is if we want to experience God's power, we should express more of our praise to him. If God is present in our praises, so is his power. Power for joy comes from living a life of praise.

With your indulgence, I'll close this chapter with another little story.

In the early 1980's I was the pastor of a small country church near Spokane, Washington. My family and I lived about two miles from the church. We had a menagerie of pets, including some horses, chickens, and goats. The children thrived on the freedom of country living and caring for their animals. It was a good life.

I owned a 1969 Ford F-250 pickup truck which I used to haul feed and firewood, tow our horse trailer, and transport other bulky items. The truck needed some service, so one morning I drove into town to an automotive shop. Ruth picked me up in our car and would bring me back when the truck was ready. Several hours later the mechanic called saying the work was done. We headed to town again. She dropped me off at the shop and left to care for some other errands she needed to run.

I stepped to the counter and the mechanic handed me the bill. I couldn't believe my eyes when I saw the bottom line! It was far more than I expected. Beyond reason!

When I objected (rather vigorously) he simply replied, "Well, we're not a discount shop here."

I was livid. There was nothing I could do but write the check, collect my keys, and head for home. I don't know when I've been so angry. Money was tight already without being severely overcharged for a couple of simple service items for my truck! It just wasn't right!

But then, on the way home, the Lord started whispering his grace in my ear. This time his grace challenged my attitude.

"Okay Lord," I said, "I know what I'm feeling right now is not what you would be feeling if this happened to you. Please take my angry spirit away and replace it with your joy and peace."

I began to sing . . .

Praise God from whom all blessings flow.

Praise him all creatures here below.

Praise him above ye heavenly hosts.

Praise Father, Son, and Holy Ghost!

The first time singing this doxology as I stormed along on the winding country road toward home, my voice was angry and filled with resentment. I literally yelled and growled the words, spitting them out through clenched teeth and a rigid jaw.

I sang the short hymn again.

The second time through I began to feel calmer and less upset. The third time I began to feel his peace. The fourth time I sang for joy!

The joy of the Lord became my strength in the moment of need.

As you build your spiritual firewall every morning you will be fortified with God's power by finding your joy in him and discovering his joy in you.

There is victory in Jesus.

Chapter Five
Strength for My Body

That My Physical Well-being will Testify of God's Grace

Dear friend, I pray that you may enjoy good health and that all may go well with you, even as your soul is getting along well (3 John 2).

Those who wait on the Lord shall renew their strength; they shall mount up with wings like eagles, they shall run and not be weary, they shall walk and not faint (Isaiah 40:31 NKJV).

If the Spirit of him who raised Jesus from the dead dwells in you, he who raised Christ from the dead will also give life to your mortal bodies through his Spirit who dwells in you (Romans 8:11).

My childhood physician, Dr. Frank Shearer lived for 107 years.

When National Geographic Magazine ran an article featuring regions of the world where large percentages of the population live past 100 years—places known as "Blue Zones"—Dr. Frank's picture appeared with him on water skis at age one-hundred-and-one! That was in

September 2005. I was excited to see someone from "my world" show up in that prestigious journal.

Quite a few years before that, our paths had crossed at a cowboy campmeeting where I discovered he was an avid horseman, something I did not know previously. I hadn't seen him in nearly 30 years. He was about 94 or 95 then.

Dr. Frank's entire life was adventure, discovery, and generosity. In 1925 he began practicing medicine in the tiny agricultural community of Toppenish, Washington. During the Great Depression years of the 1930s, payment for his services often came in the form of fruit, vegetables, or a chicken. He did house calls and never refused service to anyone for lack of funds.

Besides his patients—and those horses—he also loved water sports, fishing, hunting, and hiking the trails of the Pacific Northwest. Through the years he owned several airplanes and loved to fly when he was called upon to travel. He lived his life to serve and encourage others. Dr. Frank Shearer was an incredible human being. I have only recently grown to appreciate what a privilege and honor it was to be one of his many patients.

How did he do it? What kind of spirit drives a man to live that long with his never-ending passion for life? What wellspring provides such a fountain of vibrant longevity? Is it something all the rest of us can find, as well?

I love the story someone told during former President George H. W. Bush's funeral, reporting that he once said, "The goal is to die young as old as possible!" President Bush was 94 when he died. He kept his upbeat attitude to the very end. What a great example for us all.

Sadly, we've all heard stories about people who retire, get bored, and soon die just sitting in the easy chair. Who wants to end up like that? No one! Certainly not me. And, I suspect, not you either.

Every day is a new day with God. The *Seven Essential Daily Prayers* have been revolutionary for my walk with the Creator/Redeemer/King. That's why I have felt so called to share them with everyone I can. I covet this rich spiritual walk for every person reading this book. I really hope the idea of these priority prayers will impact your life as profoundly as they have mine.

The focus of prayer in this chapter is "Strength for My Body." I'm going to spend the bulk of the time here talking about the amazing machine that God has designed for our earthly residence. But before we begin there are two disclaimers I need to put right upfront.

> *First, even though I'll be covering a lot of detail with general information about the human body and healthful living practices, the core message here is our relationship to the Creator, his purpose for giving us life, and our part in keeping mind and body in good working order.*

> *Second, I am neither an expert nor authority in the arenas of physical health and wellbeing. I can't—and don't—claim any advanced training in these areas. The closest I come to that is an earned under-graduate academic minor in HPE&R (Health, Physical Education, and Recreation).*

> *The health of our bodies bears a direct relationship to*

both mental and spiritual wellness. Both suffer when our body is sick, weak, or exhausted. To find optimal strength mentally and spiritually, we need to treat the body the best we can for the best health we can achieve. The material in this chapter is presented with that ideal in mind.

I heard a funny story several years ago. It seems a fellow was hiking in the Appalachian Mountains when he noticed a lot of smoke curling into the sky above a ridge just ahead. He ran up the trail to find the fire. As he rounded a corner and came over the summit, he saw a cabin with the back porch nearly engulfed in flames. He rushed to see what he might do to help. When he got closer, he saw an old mountain man sitting on the front porch leaning back in his rocking chair casually smoking a corncob pipe.

"Hey!" the hiker yelled. "Your house is on fire!"

The old-timer looked up, slowly took another puff on his pipe and drawled, "Yeah, I know. I been sittin' here prayin' about that."

Okay. Now that you've probably chuckled at that little tale, let's apply it to real life.

Praying is good. We should always pray about all our troubles. But many times—especially in the arenas of health and wellness—the answers we get are directly related to our choice of actions. Putting healthy habits to work with our prayers will generally get more desirable results than simply praying and not acting. It's just the way things are.

Here's a simple concept: *We are **stewards** of God's*

gifts of life, health, and strength.

A steward is a caretaker of someone else's belongings.

Imagine a medieval estate. Somewhere on the property stands a great house or maybe a castle. That is the home of the "Lord of the Manor" and his immediate family. The manor would typically be staffed with many household servants charged with various responsibilities like cleaning, cooking, serving meals, doing the laundry, and whatever else needed attention. At a distance from the main house would be various carriage houses, barns, sheds, etc. There would be pens and shelters for keeping animals—horses, cows, sheep, pigs, etc. The buildings might even include living quarters for the hired servants who cared for this part of the lord's enterprises.

> **Key Concept:**
> *Caring for our personal health reveals love and appreciation for the Creator who gives us everything.*

In Middle-English a pen for the animals was called a "sty" as in "pigsty." The word was used for the pens of other animals as well as pigs. The hired servant in charge of the sty and the animals it held was called a "sty-warden." Now, centuries later, those two words have merged together creating our current word "steward."

The steward did not own the animals himself. He was only charged with their care. He was accountable to his employer, the Lord of the Manor, who was the actual owner.

In our case, God is the ultimate Owner of Everything,

even including the body housing our life here on Earth. He has created us and redeemed us, so we are twice his. People who say, "It's my body. I can do with it what I please," totally miss the mark. If we accept the premise that our body is designed and created by God, and he lovingly provides it for our earthly existence, then it really belongs to him.

We are stewards of this magnificent gift. He gives us the freedom to do as we will with it, but if we accept that everything ultimately belongs to him, we will honor him with our entire self—body, mind, and spirit.

King David of Ancient Israel understood the incredible wonder of the human body. In one of his most beautiful song-poems he wrote, "I praise you because I am fearfully and wonderfully made; your works are wonderful, I know full well" (Psalm 139:14).

Let's take a quick look at a few of the fully integrated, synchronized systems built into our body.

Musculoskeletal System:

There is a fun story told by the Old Testament prophet Ezekiel about his vision of an entire valley filled with hundreds of dry bones[17]. The Lord tells Ezekiel to prophesy to the bones so he (God) can restore the life of all those dead soldiers. Ezekiel does as he is told, then writes, "there was a noise, and suddenly a rattling; and the bones came together, bone to bone" (Ezekiel 37:7 NKJV).

---

[17] Read the story in Ezekiel 37:1-14.

Imagine the action! *Clackety-clack, rattle, rattle, snap, crackle, pop, pop, pop!* That must have made Ezekiel's hair stand on end! And, it must have gone on for quite a while, too.

All those dry bones assembled themselves into bare skeletons. Sinews, muscles, and tendons began covering the bones, and finally, skin provided the outside layer of each body. The Lord then tells Ezekiel to command the breath of life to come from the four winds of heaven, saying, "Come from the four winds, O breath, and breathe into these slain, that they may live" (verse 9). Ezekiel prophesies again and the corpses come to life and stand to their feet, a great army!

(If you're like me, about now you have that old Negro spiritual playing in your head—"Dem bones, dem bones, dem dry bones . . . Now hear the word of the Lord!")

Let's look a little closer at our own not-so-dry bones.

An adult human body normally has 206 bones, each with its own specialized function. Most of us rarely think consciously about our bones. These organs which provide the basic platform of our physical existence are far more complex than simple foundation parts supporting the rest of body functions.

- The long bones of the legs and arms, the pelvis, ribs, sternum, and vertebrae are hollow, containing marrow for producing blood cells.

- The tiny bones in the ear—the hammer, anvil, and stirrup—enable hearing by converting sound vibrations in the air into electrical signals for transmission to the hearing center of our brain via the aural nerve.

- Each hand is composed of twenty-seven (27!) bones perfectly arranged to articulate incredibly complex motions, giving humans quantum superiority over all other creatures on earth to develop unique cultural expressions.

On top of and attached to the bones are muscles and tendons arranged in a masterful, functional order. Flexors and extensors move the limbs, control posture, keep the body composed and stabilized, and enable us to walk upright on two legs. Tough, strap-like tendons from the muscles attach to their partner bones in strategic locations so when the muscle contracts the bones move.

Depending on how the muscles are counted, there are somewhere between 640-850 of them in your body. Some muscles like the heart and intestines have other, specialized functions, but every single muscle is there for a purpose.

The marvelous Musculoskeletal System is beyond amazing.

Respiratory System:

Breathing is pretty basic.

A person may live several weeks without food, perhaps a few days without water, but only a matter of minutes without air. Immediately after being born the very first thing a baby must do is start breathing. At the end of life—whenever it comes—we often refer to that last moment as, "He drew his last breath."

Although the number of in-and-out breaths per minute while resting varies significantly from infants to adults, a general average of around 12 will work for us here. Do the math: 12 breaths/minute x 60 minutes=720 breaths in an hour, 17,280 breaths per 24 hours, 6,307,200 breaths a year, and over 441.5 million breaths in a lifetime of 70 years! Along the way, we might experience colds, touches of flu, pneumonia, cancer, toxic fumes, overheated rooms, or freezing temps, but so long as life lasts our lungs and related equipment just keep working away non-stop, night and day, day in and day out, asleep or awake. It boggles the mind.

The breathing "equipment" is impressive.

- Two lungs reside in the chest near the spine. The right lung has three lobes and is slightly larger than the left which shares space with the heart and accommodates that need by having only two lobes instead of three. Together the two lungs weigh (on average) close to three pounds.

- The lungs have a concave (inwardly curved) lower surface which sits on the domed diaphragm muscle separating the chest from the abdomen. As the diaphragm pulls downward it expands the lungs, drawing air through the breathing passageways into the interior. This is the action that continuously repeats automatically night and day, keeping us alive even when we are asleep or unconscious.

- Within the lungs, the air passageways divide into smaller and smaller tubes and tubules until they reach the microscopic level where tiny balloon-shaped "alveoli" wait to work their magic. The total distance of all airways added together is more than 1,200 miles, with 300-500 *million* alveoli at the ends of those channels.

- Alveoli are the working "boots on the ground" soldiers of respiration. Incoming air is rich in oxygen which body cells need for oxidizing nutritional fuel into useful energy. Alveoli grab oxygen molecules from inhaled air and transfer them to red cell carriers in the bloodstream, which in turn deliver those same oxygen molecules to their destination cells. The red blood cells then pick up discarded carbon dioxide cells, transport them back to the lungs, and deliver them to the alveoli which release them into the air for exhalation. All of this process, of course, takes place a matter of mere seconds. While you are reading this, consciously take in a deep breath and immediately exhale. That's the speed of these transfers. Oxygen in. CO_2 out. Over and over. Every time you breathe. Over 6.3 million times a year.

Methinks we should really be kind to these tiny "foot-soldiers" for all they do to keep us healthy and happy. They deserve our respect and support.

Circulatory System:

Sometime during my seventh-grade year, our school showed a new hour-long "made for TV" film, "Hemo the Magnificent."[18] This mixed animation/live-action movie

---

[18] To watch "Hemo the Magnificent" on YouTube, go to **https://www.youtube.com** and do a search for the film title.

illustrated complex scientific workings of the heart, lungs, arteries, and veins carrying blood throughout the body. It featured the role of hemoglobin—aka "Hemo"—carrying oxygen from the lungs out to the body and bringing CO_2 back for disposal. Bear in mind, this movie was made over 60 years ago in 1957, but it is still today a masterful story of the inner workings of the circulatory system. Even young children can understand the message.

The "heart" of our body's circulation system is the heart muscle itself. *Lub-dub, lub-dub, lub-dub,* this four-chambered living pump repeats its action over and over, resting only momentarily between every beat. Barring disease, accident, or some other unfortunate incident, this miracle muscle continues without interruption for a lifetime of service.

Since "Hemo the Magnificent" was first aired, scientific knowledge of heart functions has exploded with ever-increasing new understanding. Today, open heart surgeries, valve replacements, multiple by-pass operations, even complete heart transplants are common. Those medical procedures were unimaginable when "Hemo" first appeared on screen.

The purpose of the heart pump and the entire circulation system is to supply oxygen and nutrient-rich blood to the body and carry away impurities and waste. Without blood flowing through the vessels death quickly arrives. I personally know how dangerous a significant loss of blood can be. Twice in my lifetime, I have come close to bleeding out. Only miracles preserved my life on each occurrence.

When I was 11 years old, I was severely injured in an accident with my American Saddlebred mare. We tumbled backward over the side of a small bridge when she reared in fear. My body was crushed against the ends of two rusty bolts as we fell onto a large wooden water pipe used for irrigation. Those two bolts penetrated my left side, broke a rib, and punctured a lung. If it had not been for a neighbor girl, Janet Mason, I would never have survived. She just "happened" to see the accident, and her quick action saved my life. The black stains of my blood stayed on those bolts for many years until the old wooden pipe was replaced by a new one made of stainless steel. I would have "bled out" right there on the spot, but by the grace of God and Janet's quick thinking, I lived to see many more days. As you can well imagine, quite a few blood transfusions were needed to restore and preserve my life.[19]

The second incident involved a bleeding GERD ulcer when I was in my early 50's. That one took 5 units and an overnight hospital stay to get me back up to speed. The miracle here was advanced medical knowledge, skilled hospital workers, and readily available supplies of blood and medicine.

I've learned to take nothing for granted. Any breakdown of the system at any point would have spelled my doom. I am grateful and thank God for every blessing.

And my heart still carries on. *Lub-dub, lub-dub, lub-dub.* Thank you, Lord!

---

[19] You can read this story in its entirety in my book "Whoa! I Yelled, 'Whoa!" available from **https://www.amazon.com**. A search for "Loren L. Fenton" will take you to my author page on Amazon.

Nervous System:

The heart and lungs are not the only organs in your body that work around the clock for you. Your brain is—quite literally—the most sophisticated, powerful computer to be found anywhere on Planet Earth. It never sleeps, even when you do! In recent decades, great strides have been made in understanding the inner workings of this small organ.

Take strokes, for example.

Back in the mid-1950s, my mother's aunt suffered a severe stroke. No one back then even came close to understanding the cause. Strokes were shrouded in deep mystery, the stuff of old wives' tales, spooky myths, and scary legends.

My great-aunt's post-stroke life was bizarre and sometimes funny. I found her antics both terrifying and entertaining. Even the term "stroke" implied that something supernatural or evil had touched her brain and messed up her mind.

I was afraid of her. The adults of our extended family were confused and saddened by her condition.

Today we know so much more! Causes of strokes can be blood clots, tumors, or brain trauma. Doctors now have the knowledge and ability to immediately reverse the effects if they have a timely opportunity and the right conditions. It is truly wonderful what modern medicine can do.

With your brain serving as "information connection central," the entire human nervous system is beyond incredible.

Have you ever had a tiny, almost invisible sliver stuck in your finger? How did you know it was there? You could feel it, of course! Every time you picked something up, or brushed your hand against a doorknob, or lifted a piece of paper, that nearly microscopic sticker reminded you it was there, and it wasn't going away. In fact, I'd guess it may have been so irritating you finally had to drop everything else so you could focus all your attention on getting it removed. Once it was gone you could get back to business and forget it was ever a problem.

Here's something amazing about this little scenario. As your brain processed pain from that tiny spot on your finger, you knew exactly—with perfect precision—where to look to find it.

Trillions of nerve cells throughout your body stream unbroken statuses up to headquarters, which continuously monitors every square micro-millimeter of your person. So long as you live, the nervous super-highway never stops zinging messages to and from your brain. It's pretty much how you know you are alive.

Our wonderful bodies have many more systems working non-stop—in perfect synchronization—with those we've explored above. Nevertheless, from just the few we have looked at we can see how incredibly complex and beautiful God made this earthly house we often take so much for granted.

The Apostle Paul said, "In [God] we live and move and have our being" (Acts 17:28).

God himself is the source of our strength. The Holy Spirit living in our heart energizes our physical body and gives us life. "If the Spirit of him who raised Jesus from the dead dwells in you, he who raised Christ from the dead will also give life to your mortal bodies through his Spirit who dwells in you" (Romans 8:11). Knowing this, it is entirely appropriate for one of our essential daily prayers to be "strength for my body."

I personally feel great assurance when I wake up every morning realizing my life is empowered by the ever-present Spirit of the living God.

Here is an important truth, however: Becoming aware of the majesty and magnificence of our being is only the first step. As God does his part, we also have a responsibility. If we are serious about *praying* for strength, the next step is to *choose life practices* that are known to provide optimal health and well-being. Remember, we are stewards—caretakers—of this inestimable gift of God's grace, our body.

How do we do that? How do we choose the best? How do we live as faithful and responsible stewards?

Here are some suggestions:

1. Start with a good attitude (You might want to go back and read Chapter 4, "Joy in My Spirit" again.)

2. Follow a healthful lifestyle

3. Educate yourself in basic principles of healthful living

4. Avoid fads and extremes

5. Incorporate natural, common-sense practices into your daily life—like these:

1. Diet

Science and an ever-growing body of testimonial evidence suggest that a mostly plant-based food plan works best for weight control, muscle strength, energy management, mental alertness, and a host of other benefits.

One excellent source of information and documentation is the *Forks Over Knives Plan: How to Transition to the Life-Saving, Whole-Food, Plant-Based Diet* by Alona Pulde, MD, and Matthew Lederman, MD. I highly recommend that you check out their website[20].

2. Water

Water is the most common compound found on our planet. All life as we know it is dependent on this amazing molecule—two hydrogen atoms bonded to one of oxygen, aka "H_2O."

Human bodies average between 50-75% water, depending on age, body mass, and gender. Overweight people tend to have less body-water than more fit individuals because fat contains less water than lean muscle. Men's bodies generally have a larger percentage of water than women, due to the fact that women typically carry more fat than men. Babies' bodies can be up to 75% water.[21]

---

[20] Full information on this plan is available at **https://www.forksoverknives.com/**. (Disclaimer: I have received no compensation, material or otherwise, from this organization, or any other referenced source throughout this book. I include them here because I personally have found them helpful and beneficial.)

How much water intake should you have each day? Recent guidelines recommend *your body weight (lbs.) divided by two*. Drink that many ounces of water every 24 hours. Example: A person weighing 150 lbs. should take in 75 ounces of fluid every day—around 8-9 8oz glasses per day. With that simple formula, you can do the math for your personal needs.

3. Exercise

I must confess—a productive exercise program is hard for me to follow with reasonable consistency. No excuses. I just struggle with making it happen on a regular, daily basis. My doctor makes a point to remind me of what I should be doing every time I see him.

Not to worry, I have a plan.

I recently purchased an activity tracker—a Fitbit Charge 3. This little wrist-band device will be my "exercise-diet-sleep-weight monitor-water intake-and-calorie counter" from now until some unknown future date when I may deem it no longer necessary. Quite frankly, I am looking forward to the journey using this thing. It appears to be a good fit for giving me the extra nudge I need. The goal is 10,000-12,000 steps a day. Reaching that milestone will be a day for me to celebrate, for sure!

A word of caution: If you decide to start an exercise program, you need to first counsel with your personal health-care professional. Too many people have run into serious physical problems without realizing the danger

---

[21] https://www.thoughtco.com/how-much-of-your-body-is-water-609406

they could bring upon themselves by starting too fast, overdoing it, and end up paying a huge, unexpected and unwanted price. For some, the price has been sudden death. Don't let that happen to you. Talk to your doctor. First.

Why be concerned about exercise? Because it is part of being in the best health possible. It is all about the stewardship factor. It is one more way we can testify to the greatness of our awesome Creator God.

4.   Rest/Sleep

I love a good night's sleep—and naps! I inherited my mother's ability to take a 15-20-minute nap and wake up refreshed and ready to continue whatever I was doing. Not everyone can do the power nap thing, but it works for me. If you can, try zoning out for a quick few minutes in the middle of your day. It may give you just the boost you need for finishing an important task.

Have you ever thought about the business side of sleep? It is huge! A quick online check reveals that current estimates (2019) indicate the annual sleep-health industry may be worth between $60-$80 *billion* dollars in the United States alone. Bedroom furniture and decor, comfortable sleepwear, soothing bath and beauty products, prescription medications, and OTC sleep aids are just a few of the many items Americans buy every day hoping to improve their sleep.

The quality of a person's waking hours is directly affected by the length and depth of recent sleep time. Productivity at work, focus at study, skill at play, recreational activities, personal relationships at home or in the office are just a few areas of everyday life that benefit from healthy, timely sleep.[22]

Getting enough sleep is vital for health, overall wellness, and productivity. So is taking a periodic rest-break during your waking hours.

In his blockbuster book *The 7 Habits of Highly Effective People,*[23] author Stephen R. Covey lists "Sharpening the Saw: Principles of Balanced Self-Renewal" as the one personal habit that keeps all the rest functioning at optimal levels. Dr. Covey uses the illustration of cutting wood with a dull saw vs. a sharp saw. The worker who takes time away from actual cutting to keep his tool sharp is much more efficient—aka "productive"—in both the amount of wood cut and the energy needed to cut it. Granted, most of us aren't woodcutters, but the principle remains. Taking time for rest and renewal will generally increase our energy for the task at hand as well as the output of our efforts.

The same principle applies on a broader scale as well. Being raised as a Seventh-day Adventist, I was taught from my earliest days about the value of a weekly sabbath—a day of rest. At the time of Creation, God gave the Sabbath as a very special gift to all humanity.[24] Later, the Lord even included his Sabbath gift as one of the Ten

---

[22] The opposite factor of fatigue is a major issue. Check out this website: https://www.nsc.org/work-safety/safety-topics/fatigue

[23] Covey, Stephen R., The 7 Habits of Highly Effective People: Restoring the Character Ethic. Simon & Schuster (Fireside Book), New York, 1989.

[24] See Genesis 2:1-3; Exodus 20:8-11

Commandments given to the Israelites through Moses on Mt. Sinai. God—our Creator—knew that human beings would work best, live longer, and be happier with a weekly routine, including an entire day when secular and business concerns could be set aside, allowing us to focus on personal peace, healthy relationships, and spiritual growth.

Try it! It works!

5. Sunshine

I think I might understand a tiny bit about why ancient cultures worshiped the sun—the most important of all gods in the pantheon of many tribes around the world. Appeasement of 'gods" and 'goddesses" to acquire benefits like food, fertility, good luck, and good health were a primary driving factor of life. Sacrificing to the "gods" was commonplace.

With the sun being the foremost deity in most religious cultures, it was natural to put him—always a male deity—at the head of every list, even giving him first place in the days of the week, e.g. the "*sun's*-day." The first day of every week became a day of worship and celebration honoring the sun—and all the benefits it brings to the earth—long before the arrival of Christianity.

The ancients believed that the sun made everything possible—from rains watering their fields, to the growth of crops, to the abundance of game, to providing the light of day overcoming the darkness of night. In their minds, the sun-god was to be worshiped so he would continue to bless them with what they needed.

In a way, they were right.

So far as the physical mechanics of the solar system is concerned, the sun does—in fact—make nearly everything happen here on Earth. The miracles of photosynthesis, for instance, could not occur without sunshine. Without photosynthesis, there would be no green plants. Without plants, there would be no food for humans or animals. There would be no fossil fuels to drive our cars, or firewood to burn in the fireplace, let alone timber with which to frame our houses. Without sunshine, there would be no evaporation from the oceans, no clouds to water the land, no wind to carry the waters over the land, no rivers for hydro-electric power or for fish to swim.

In short, sunshine is the powerhouse factor driving every natural action in the world. Without sunshine, there is no life as we know it. Not even our own.

Sunshine also does marvelous things in our bodies. For instance, sunlight with adequate amounts of UV-B radiation interacts with a type of cholesterol in our skin to produce cholecalciferol (AKA vitamin D3). Proper levels of vitamin D3 contribute to improved bone density, brain health, a stronger immune system, weight control, and lower occurrences of autoimmune diseases.[25]

If you are unsure of how much vitamin D3 you have, ask your doctor to order a blood chemistry panel for analysis. Once you have that information you can move ahead with any corrective protocol, if it may be needed. The winter sun, in latitudes further from the equator, does

---

[25] A quick online search for the benefits of vitamin D3 will provide a great volume of information on this subject.

rays needed for your skin to
so some supplementation may be
your doctor.

on:

r had an extremely bad sunburn?
Exposure to too much sun radiation can do serious
damage to your skin. While you need the sun on your
skin for its benefits, overdoing it can harm the cells and
eventually result in skin cancer. Balance and moderation
are the keys to health in this and all other lifestyle
practices—with a few notable exceptions.

6. Temperance

Sometime along in my teen years, our church youth
leaders handed out a "Temperance Pledge" and
encouraged all of us to sign it so we could carry it as a
ready reminder of our personal commitment to sobriety
and healthful living. The Pledge read something like this:

> Realizing the importance of healthy body
> and mind, I promise, with the help
> of God, to live a Christian life of true
> temperance in all things and to abstain
> from the use of tobacco, alcohol, or any
> other narcotic.

Along with all the other young people in the group, I
gladly and willingly signed the card which I kept in my
wallet for many years. Somewhere along the way, it
disappeared, but I didn't need it in my pocket. The
message was written deep in my heart.

Part of my family heritage is anything but pretty. In the

early 20th century my father's family moved from Missouri/Kansas to northern Idaho where my grandfather found work in the silver-lead ore mines. Orofino was a rough town, filled with hardscrabble miners and loggers. In those days, alcohol flowed like water in the saloons and bars.

After only a few short years my grandfather Arthur Fenton became a severe alcoholic. One tragic day in 1907, he ran away from his family and didn't return. It was decades before his family saw him again. My dad was 11 years old.

That one act created chaos in the Fenton family. Its echoes still rumble more than a century later.

My father and his three sisters—mere children at the time—were each "farmed out" to foster families. Grandma did the best she could but simply could not support them alone. The girls became bitter and resentful toward their father. Their brother—my dad—struggled with abandonment issues for years. Because of alcohol's evil effects on the family and on himself, he refused to drink it in any form, ever. He cursed it until the day he died.

I was never tempted to drink. I knew the generational history. I knew it wasn't good. I wanted no part of it.

Another sad spin-off of that abandonment, however, was that my father started smoking almost immediately afterward. From age 11 until he died at age 75, King Nicotine owned his lungs. Throughout all my growing-up years, nearly every night a nasty smoker's cough racked my dad's body as he struggled to clear the mucus and phlegm from his throat.

Emphysema eventually took his life.

LOREN L FENTON

I saw the first-hand bitter fruit of smoking, upfront and personal. No way did I want that for myself. So, signing the Temperance Pledge was a no-brainer for me. I had neither need nor desire to travel those roads of destruction.

Traditionally, temperance was defined as "total abstinence from that which is harmful; moderation in that which is good." But, I recently made what I considered a thrilling discovery.

The biblical Greek word *egkrateia* (pronounced "eng-kra-TIA") is rendered as "moderation" or "temperance" in most English translations, carrying a rather milk-toast implication of "balance," or "just a little bit is okay." However, *egkrateia* carries much more force than that!

What it really means is *true mastery from within!* Genuine *egkrateia* embodies the concepts of total self-control, self-discipline, self-mastery, and self-restraint. It could be defined as "true personal righteousness."

The trouble with this, of course, is that reaching this state of personal mastery is completely impossible in the strength of our own flesh. If *egkrateia* equates to personal righteousness—which it does—the Bible is clear: we don't have it and can't get it on our own. Isaiah 64:6 says, "All our righteous acts are like filthy rags." In other words, even the good things we attempt are all tainted with the poison of self-centeredness and sin.

Egkrateia is a spiritual fruit of God's Spirit dwelling in our hearts.[26] Praying for strength for our body, then, is to pray for the Holy Spirit's gift of *true mastery from within,*

---

[26] See Galatians 5:22-23

82

enabling us to choose—and live—a healthy life of energy and vitality for the glory of God.

7. Fresh Air

Every time I visit a doctor for a check-up the attending nurse clips a little device to one of my fingertips. This small clip measures and reports the amount of oxygen in my blood. A saturation reading above 97% is good; less than 90% sets off alarms.

The low oxygen content can result from a variety of conditions and cause serious damage to our body. Internal organs can fail, brain function slows or ceases, and general functions become impaired or fail.

On the other hand, consider the joy of filling your lungs with a deep breath of cool fresh air after being stuck for hours in a stuffy, over-heated room! Wonderful, isn't it? When I was a youngster my friends and I could never decide if it "felt good," or "tasted good." I still haven't figured that one out. It was awesome whatever you called it.

There's a good reason it feels so great. The oxygen we get in fresh air does amazing things for us. Take a low intensity walk outside after a meal. The exercise stimulates your heart and increases your circulation. Your breathing rate increases, delivering a larger volume of oxygen to the body cells.

Oxygen aids in digestion and benefits vital functions like blood pressure and heart rate. Processing oxygen helps produce serotonin—a body hormone that makes you feel happier and more content. Your white blood cells—the disease defenders—are fired by oxygen to fight and kill harmful bacteria, bolstering your immune system.

Getting adequate oxygen also helps you think more clearly, boosts your energy levels, and helps you concentrate. Breathing all that fresh air cleanses your lungs, expands the airways, and expels body toxins like carbon dioxide (CO_2).

In terms of a current slang expression, fresh air is some incredible "awesome sauce!"

Where do we get this magic mixture of breathable beneficence? Go outdoors, out of the city. Go to a park, a nature preserve, to the beach, to the mountains, or a forest. Anywhere away from the smog and air pollution. If you live in a place of little pollution, open your bedroom windows at night and enjoy the refreshing night breezes.

If all this is impractical or unavailable to you, invest in an air filtering machine for your living quarters. Many brands and styles are available. They not only filter dust and other impurities, but some are also equipped to sanitize the air, making it healthier for you to breathe. The better the quality of the air around you, the better it can serve your body's health requirements.

A clear mind, clean lungs, and great energy are powerful factors for positive, praise-filled living. God's gift of fresh air for our world is a major factor making that possible.

8.   Trust in Divine Power

One day during my sophomore year in college I

opened my dorm mailbox and was delighted to see an envelope with my sister's return address printed in the corner. Opening it, I discovered a small card with this printed text: "Trust in the Lord with all your heart and lean not on your own understanding; in all your ways acknowledge him, and he shall direct your paths" (Proverbs 3:5-6 NKJV). That promise has been precious to me through all the years since then. God is good!

Can God be trusted? Absolutely. Without a doubt.

I wish I could say that my trust in God has been one unbroken journey, moving forward from faith to faith. Sadly, I cannot. There have been way too many times when I presumptively jumped ahead of his leading or turned off of the highway to heaven chasing some elusive fantasy.

Not long after I gave my heart to the Lord at age 16, I discovered a Bible promise that became a lifelong "touchstone" text for me: "Have I not commanded you? Be strong and courageous. Do not be terrified; do not be discouraged, for the Lord your God will be with you wherever you go" (Joshua 1:9).

The moment I read that statement—which God made to Joshua assuring him of success in the task ahead—I knew I could also claim it as my own. I did, and the Lord has kept his side of the deal with me, just as he promised Joshua and was faithful to him in the conquest of Canaan.

I can truthfully say that even on days when I wandered off the path and turned my focus elsewhere, he never abandoned either me or his word.

You can depend on God.

Trusting God's providence is better than living in fear of an unknown tomorrow.

Trusting God's love is better than fearing his punishment.

Trusting God's peace is better than fighting the storms of life without shelter.

Trusting God's presence is better than weeping in the shadows of loneliness and loss.

Trusting God's light is better than cursing the darkness.

Trusting God's strength is better than succumbing to human weaknesses of body, mind, or spirit.

Trusting God's salvation is better than dying without hope for a better tomorrow.

Trusting God is just a better way to live.

I close this chapter with another text of divine instruction from the Apostle Paul. "Therefore, whether you eat or drink, or whatever you do, do all to the glory of God" (1 Corinthians 10:31).

Amen.

Chapter Six

Wisdom for My Counsel

That the Fear of the Lord Might ever be My Guide

God grant me the SERENITY to accept things I cannot change; The COURAGE to change things I can; and the WISDOM to know the difference.[27]

The quiet words of the wise are more to be heeded than the shouts of a ruler of fools. Wisdom is better than weapons of war (Ecclesiastes 9:17-18).

      I never had the privilege of sitting at the feet of Dr. Edward Heppenstall, one of the most influential Seventh-day Adventist theologians of the 20th century. When I arrived at the theological seminary at Andrews University in 1998, Dr. Heppenstall had already transferred to teach for a few years at Loma Linda University before retirement. A good friend and colleague

---

[27] This "Serenity Prayer" is used in many 12-step programs such as Alcoholics Anonymous.

of mine did attend his classes at Andrews, however. My friend often quoted a statement he attributed to Dr. Heppenstall's lectures: He said, "The mark of a mature mind is to withhold judgment until all the facts are in."

It occurs to me that we could nicely paraphrase that thought to say, "The mark of wisdom is to get as much information as possible before jumping to conclusions."

Let's look at something Jesus said: "Behold, I send you forth as sheep in the midst of wolves: be ye therefore wise (Greek: *phrónimos*) as serpents, and harmless as doves" (Matthew 10:16 KJV). Many modern versions translate the Greek word *phrónimos* as "shrewd," as in "shrewd as serpents." A quick check of an analytical concordance shows some other possibilities. Personally, I like "prudent," "judicious," "well-advised," "sensible," and "cautious."

> **Key Concept:**
> *True wisdom follows neither the capricious fads of populism nor the immobility of frozen traditionalism.*

In other words, Jesus told his disciples to use some common sense when dealing with people who might appear friendly but who hide their true intentions. That sounds like "wisdom" to me.

Simon Peter's brother John echoed Jesus' teaching in his first letter to the believers, "Dear friends, do not believe every spirit, but test the spirits to see whether they are from God" (1 John 4:1). Think, analyze, consider. Don't be naive or gullible. Get all the facts. Then, act accordingly.

The ever-analytical and always eloquent Apostle Paul made this fascinating observation: "Jews demand miraculous signs and Greeks look for wisdom, but we preach Christ crucified: a stumbling block to Jews and foolishness to Gentiles, but to those whom God has called, both Jews and Greeks, Christ the power of God and the wisdom of God" (1 Corinthians 1:22-25).

We need to take a closer look at Paul's statement.

In the Old Testament Hebrew language, the word for "wisdom" was *chokmah*. This word carried several meanings or implications. For instance, *chokmah* could mean skill in war, wisdom in administration, shrewdness, prudence in religious affairs, or insight for ethical and religious settings. The specific meaning had to be understood from the context of the surrounding text.

In the 1st century A.D. during the time of Jesus and later, the basis of Jewish acceptance of truth and wisdom was any kind of supernatural sign. The Jews repeatedly asked Jesus, "What miraculous sign can you show us to prove your authority to do all this? (John 2:18), and "What miraculous sign will you give that we may see it and believe you? (John 6:30). These questions came both from the leaders (scribes, Pharisees, etc.) and from the common people who were schooled by the teachings of the priests.

When Jesus didn't give them such a sign, many no longer followed him. They couldn't accept a "prophet" who refused to entertain them with the "miracles" they wanted to see.

The Greeks, on the other hand—whose developing cultural timeline roughly parallels that of ancient Israel—looked for wisdom from their philosophers. The Greek philosopher-teachers were men who "loved wisdom." Our modern word "philosophy" comes from joining two Greek words *philos* (to love) and *sophia* (wisdom).

The three most famous Greek philosophers were Socrates, Plato, and Aristotle. Following the methods of teaching pioneered by these three, the Greeks evolved an entire society dedicated to the discovery of truth through philosophical debate, discussion, and constant exploration of ideas. The Apostle Paul encountered this in his visit to Athens when he met with some of these "scholars" on Mars Hill.

The Greek people built magnificent temples to their gods and goddesses. In the mid-fifth century B.C. the Athenians built the Parthenon on an acropolis (Mars Hill) near their city and dedicated it to Athena, the goddess of wisdom. This was where high-minded intellectuals of the city gathered to endlessly talk philosophy. It is where Paul met with them and delivered one of the greatest speeches recorded in Scripture.[28]

Thus, Paul knew from personal experience about both the Jews and the Greeks in their respective search for wisdom. Paul's assertion is that neither way is adequate. Look again at what he said.

"Jews demand miraculous signs and Greeks look for wisdom, but *we preach Christ crucified: a stumbling block to Jews and foolishness to Gentiles, but to those*

---

[28] You can read this story in Acts 17:16-34.

whom God has called, both Jews and Greeks, Christ the power of God and the wisdom of God" (1 Corinthians 1:22-25 emphasis mine).

Two thousand years ago Paul understood the futility of both foci. True wisdom can be found in neither. It can only be found in the risen Christ! The so-called "wisdom" of the world is often self-serving and characterized by shrewdness and craftiness. In the dog-eat-dog world of one-upmanship, winning at any cost is the name of the game.

Success for the Jews of Paul's day was seeing proof in the form of miracles they could see and touch, affirming their own rightness as God's chosen people. The message of a crucified Messiah simply couldn't satisfy that need. To them, the Rabbi from Nazareth was a total failure who deserved to die.

In their own way, the Greeks agreed. Call death on a Roman cross a victory? Preposterous! Death is not victory. Death in battle means total defeat.

In the middle of that argument, Paul declares with pointed force, "You're both wrong. The crucified Christ is the ultimate source of both power and wisdom!"

Contrast those Jewish and Greek ideas of wisdom—so-called—with the statements of biblical prophets who really understood the truth:

1.   "The fear of the Lord is the beginning of wisdom, and the knowledge of the Holy One is understanding" (Proverbs 9:10).

2.   "If any of you lacks wisdom, he should ask of God . . . and it will be given to him" (James 1:5).

3.   "To each [believer] the manifestation of the Spirit is given for the common good . . . the message of wisdom" (1 Corinthians 12:7-8).

4.   "The Spirit of the Lord will rest on him— that is, the "Branch," i.e. the "Messiah,"—the Spirit of wisdom and understanding" (Isaiah 11:2).

The prophets all agree: *Wisdom is a (spiritual) gift from God.*

The Bible tells of numerous individuals gifted with incredible wisdom. Two who immediately come to mind are the Old Testament stories of Joseph[29] and Daniel.[30]

Joseph—the favorite son of the Patriarch Jacob— was sold into slavery by his ten jealous brothers. He was transported to Egypt and acquired in the slave market by a high official named Potiphar. Potiphar's wife thought this young Hebrew slave looked pretty good and tried to seduce him. Joseph refused, and as a result, got thrown into prison. There, he conducted himself with such honesty and integrity that he was made overseer of all the other prisoners.

One night, two of those fellow prisoners each had a strange dream which they believed carried significant meaning, and they asked Joseph about their dreams.

---

[29] Joseph's story can be found in Genesis 37ff.

[30] Read about Daniel's experience in Daniel 1-2.

God gave Joseph supernatural insight to interpret the dreams, which proved to be prophetically accurate.

A full two years later, Pharaoh— the king of Egypt—also had two dreams he could not understand. His personal butler—one of the prison dreamers— suddenly remembered how Joseph was able to interpret his dream in prison. Pharaoh called for Joseph, who came, listened to Pharaoh's description of the dreams, and told him the meaning: seven years of plenty lay ahead for Egypt, followed by another seven years of drought and famine.

Joseph counseled Pharaoh to use the next seven years preparing for the years of famine to follow. Pharaoh liked the idea and appointed Joseph as Prime Minister of Egypt to oversee the task of storing grain so the people can survive the upcoming years of want.

The famine extended far north into the lands where Jacob and his family lived as nomadic shepherds. Joseph's brothers arrived in Egypt to buy grain, but they did not recognize Joseph, although he immediately knew them. Some interesting events transpired, and in the end, Jacob and all his household moved to Egypt to survive the famine.

Woven throughout the entire story of Joseph is a golden thread of integrity and wisdom. I believe it started as Joseph—a newly purchased prisoner-slave—gazed at his father's tents as the caravan traveled toward Egypt.

The ancient trade route from Damascus in Syria to Memphis in Egypt ran south along the eastern shore of the Mediterranean Sea through what we know today as the Gaza Strip. At the beginning of Joseph's story, he found his brothers pasturing the family flocks in northern Galilee. Their father's main camp was far to the South in the Negev. When the camel caravan passed the brothers' field camp they saw a convenient opportunity to get Joseph out of their lives and proceeded to sell him to the traders.

On the journey south, the caravan passed to the west of Jacob's tents. The young Joseph gazed at his home in the distance and realized he may never see his father or other family members again. He had no idea what his immediate future would bring. It isn't a stretch to think he must have experienced extreme confusion and fear. And, yet, as he peered across the desert toward the only home he had ever known, he resolved that regardless of what might happen to him in the future he would be true to the teachings of his father, and he would continue to worship only the God of Jacob.

Joseph made a wise choice. God honored his choice and blessed him with favor throughout the rest of his life. Every day he continued to serve those around him with true dignity, honor, and respect.

Daniel has a similar story from (roughly) a thousand years later.

A young Hebrew prince is captured along with many of his fellow countrymen and marched across the desert from Jerusalem to Babylon in 605 B.C. Daniel and three other young captives are selected for training in the "University of Babylon" in all the language and literature of Babylon's culture.

King Nebuchadnezzar wanted these young Hebrews to serve in the palace. He recognized their outstanding aptitude and promise, instructing the chief of the court officials to give them the best of food and other Babylonian delicacies as part of their training. Nebuchadnezzar truly believed he was giving them every advantage to excel.

But the four Hebrew youth knew that the king's meats and wines would dull their senses and weaken their bodies. They bargained with the steward in charge of their care to let them try their own diet of vegetables and water for ten days, then determine the results.

It worked!

The story says, "At the end of the ten days they looked healthier and better nourished than any of the young men who ate the royal food. So the guard took away their choice food and the wine they were to drink and gave them vegetables instead" (Daniel 1:15-16).

As in Joseph's story, the foundational choice these young men made at the beginning of their captivity made all the difference for the rest of their lives.

Sometime later, King Nebuchadnezzar also had a divine dream, but he had no idea what it meant, and he couldn't even remember the details. He was sure it was of great importance, however. When none of the soothsayers or magicians could tell him the dream or what it might mean, the king flew into a rage and ordered that they all be killed, and their houses destroyed!

When Daniel heard about this, he arranged to ask the king for time when he and his friends could pray about the matter. They would ask God to reveal the dream and its message. Nebuchadnezzar agreed to their request.

They prayed. God answered, and Daniel was able to tell the king of four great world empires coming in the future—Babylon, Medo-Persia, Greece, and Rome—symbolized by the image of a man made of different metals—gold, silver, bronze, and iron.

Before Daniel delivered the revelation of the dream and its meaning to Nebuchadnezzar, he praised God, saying, "[You] give wisdom to the wise and knowledge to the discerning" (Daniel 2:21). Then, when he stood before the king, he prefaced his message, "No wise man, enchanter magician or diviner can explain to the king the mystery he has asked about, but there is a God in heaven who reveals mysteries. He has shown King Nebuchadnezzar what will happen in the days to come" (Daniel 2:27).

Joseph and Daniel are just two examples of individuals who received wisdom and understanding from the Holy Spirit of God. The Bible, and indeed the entire history of humanity, is filled with many similar stories as God guided his people through challenging or uncertain times.

We can trust God to give those same gifts to us in our times of need.

King Solomon who reigned during the apex of Israel's glory days declared, "Blessed is the [person] who finds wisdom, the [one] who gains understanding, for [wisdom] is more profitable than silver and yields better returns than gold" (Proverbs 3:13-14).

The Bible teaches clearly that true wisdom is a gift from a God who desires the best for his children. Holy

Spirit-given wisdom inspires positive thinking and enables good choices. While the wisdom of the world tends to self-serving and self-centered efforts of personal promotion, the wisdom of God is self-sacrificing and focused on service to others.

This wisdom from above is freely available to those who ask for it. That's why the sixth essential daily prayer in our list is "Wisdom for My Counsel: *That the Fear of the Lord Might ever be My Guide.*"

As Solomon said, "The fear of the Lord is the beginning of wisdom, and knowledge of the Holy One is understanding" (Proverbs 9:10).

Chapter Seven

To Be a Godly Influence in the World

That My Life Will Only Count for God's Eternal Kingdom

By faith Able offered God a better sacrifice than Cain did. By faith he was commended as a righteous man, when God spoke well of his offerings. And by faith he still speaks, even though he is dead (Hebrews 11:4).

I hang my head in shame when I recall some of my words and actions in the once-upon-a-time unchangeable past. I feel even worse when I think about the effect my attitudes and conduct may have had on friends and fellow travelers. So many times, my influence was wrong-headed—definitely anything but righteous.

For years I tried hard to maintain a surface facade of being a good kid, especially around adults and girls. But just under the surface, my life was full of trash and self-centered pride. All the guys I ran with knew who I really was. The others probably did too. I suspect my "cover" was far more transparent than I imagined. Truth be told, I didn't actually think about it. I just acted differently around different sets of people. I seem to have been a bonafide hypocrite and didn't even know it!

But one night God turned his powerful spotlight on all that inner ugliness and brought me to my knees. In that moment I knew my only hope was to confess my sins and plead for forgiveness. The Bible says, "If we confess our sins, he is faithful and just and will forgive us our sins and purify us from all unrighteousness" (1 John 1:9).[31]

What a great promise! My gratitude is truly beyond words. God is good.

But, here's the thing: While God's grace and forgiveness are worthy of celebration, the effect of our words and actions doesn't just go away. The influences generated from long-forgotten events never cease to ripple across the social waters of our world. Every day we toss new "pebbles" into the "pond." Every wave from every pebble becomes a force of influence that touches every person in its path. The effects can—and often do— last for generations. The energy of those waves cannot be stopped or recalled. Once in motion, they will continue their journey, constantly passing on the good or evil fruit they carry.

Consider the following incredible story from a dark era of American history.

---

[31] Later in this chapter I relate how this text—1 John 1:9— became one of the foundation cornerstones of my faith.

In the pre-dawn darkness of a Southwest Missouri Civil War morning, a tiny newborn scrap of humanity—stuffed into a burlap bag and tied to the back of a saddle—is tossed roughly into the hands of a slave-owning German immigrant named Moses. The nameless baby and his mother Mary had been stolen days earlier in a night-time raid, possibly by a band of the infamous Quantrill's Raiders, aka Confederate "bushwhackers" who carried out guerrilla attacks on civilian targets in Missouri and Kansas.

Through an intermediary, Moses attempted to negotiate the return of Mary and her child, promising to trade his prized stallion in exchange.

Sadly, the rendezvous and transaction did not go as planned. Mary was not with the raiders when they arrived at the meeting place. The bushwhackers took the stallion and then shot Moses's wagon mare in the head, killing her instantly. One of the men threw the burlap bag in Moses's general direction then followed his gang galloping off into the night. In a desperate stretch, Moses strained to catch the bag before it hit the ground. Opening it, he discovered a tiny infant still alive.

It was Mary's baby. He immediately opened his coat and placed the child next to his own bare skin, warming him and protecting him from the elements. Clutching the baby to his chest, Farmer Moses began the long walk home.

When the war ended in 1865—and the slaves now free—Moses and his wife Susan decided to formally adopt the little boy and his older brother James so they could raise them as their own. They loved the boys and wanted to give them every advantage available for Negro children in the post-war years. They named the younger brother in honor of an American President whom they greatly admired, and gave him their own last name. That little throw-away slave child would forever afterward be known as George Washington Carver.[32]

George W. Carver's accomplishments in life are the stuff of legend. Eventually, he taught for 47 years at Booker T. Washington's Tuskegee Institute (now Tuskegee University). His experiments with peanuts and sweet potatoes, methods of crop rotation, and other improvements revolutionized agriculture in the South. By the time of his death on January 5, 1943, George's fame had spread far and wide. In 1941 *Time* Magazine labeled him "a Black Leonardo." He is one of the truly great people in American history, and one of the most powerful positive influences of modern times.

The question can legitimately be asked, Where would our culture be today without the likes of George Washington Carver?

Underlying that question, however, is a deeper, more fundamental issue. Where would George Washington Carver have been without the love and nurture of his adoptive parents, Moses and Susan Carver? Even before that, how would history have been different if Moses Carver hadn't saved the life of that tiny, insignificant slave baby one terrible night in war-ravaged Southwest Missouri?

---

[32] This story is a condensed portion of a much longer, more detailed account told by author Andy Andrews in *The Lost Choice: A Legend of Personal Discovery.* Nelson Books: A Division of Thomas Nelson Publishers, 2004.

Suffice it to say, it was the Carvers' love—the commanding influence of their life—that formed the foundation of George's character and produced the fruit of his life work. Without Moses and Susan Carver, there would be no George Washington Carver. Without George Washington Carver, we all would be the poorer.

Influence is a most powerful factor in human relationships.

> **Key Concept:**
> *When we come to the end of our earthly life, the only thing we leave behind is our influence, whether for good or evil.*

In some rare moments, we may occasionally know when our presence has made a significant difference in another person's life. Most times we have no idea. It might be days or even years later—if ever at all—that we discover how our life touched another life with significance.

In the summer of 1964, I was nineteen years old. I spent most of the long break between college quarters selling children's Bible storybooks around Salem, Oregon. Whenever I had a free weekend, I often headed north on I-5 to Portland to visit a certain student nurse who was working in one of the area hospitals. She and I had a lot of fun together. We enjoyed getting better acquainted each time we got together.

On one visit Mary[33] told me she would be going home in a couple of weeks, and invited me to go with her so I could meet her parents. That sounded great to me! I rather liked where this friendship might be leading. The trip involved a long, all-day trip on a Greyhound bus, followed by another three hours by car from the town where Mary's mother met the bus to pick us up. I was a happy camper, getting to spend all this time with a young lady I enjoyed.

We did indeed have a great weekend. Her parents were friendly and welcomed me with open arms. They were farm folk, so I felt entirely comfortable in their home. Somewhere along the way, I got an invitation to sing special music for their church worship service. I agreed, and Mary accompanied me on the piano. I sang a simple little hymn of fellowship with God as my closest friend. Everyone seemed to enjoy the music. And that was that. The weekend visit came to an end. Mary and I returned to our jobs in Oregon.

Not long afterward our lives turned in different directions, but I still carried wonderful memories of a fun-filled summer, and life moved on.

Years passed—many years, in fact.

Over twenty years later I had occasion to speak as a guest pastor in that same little church. Very few of the "old-timers" were there who could remember that one lone visit and the song I sang for special music. But one of the members approached me after my sermon.

"Do you remember singing special music when you were here?" she asked.

"Yes, of course!" I answered.

---

33 Not her real name.

"Well, I just wanted you to know what a profound impression you made on my son. He was eight or nine years old back then. He really loved the song you shared, and for years afterward, he practiced and practiced. He always said, 'I want to be able to sing just like Loren Fenton!'"

Talk about a humbling experience! What a wake-up call!

I don't think my "special music" was particularly memorable, but a young boy was influenced for years afterward because of my song.

Little, seemingly insignificant moments do make a difference in the life of people we encounter every day. You never know what a wave, a smile, a word of encouragement, or a pat on the back might do to lift someone's day. Only God can trace the effect of our presence in this world. We will never know the whole story until we get into his eternal Kingdom.

Jesus says in Matthew 12:36 that we will be judged by every little word we say, whether it is good or evil. The verdict of this judgment is directly tied to the influence of our words in the life of the people around us. Do our communications result in encouragement, hope, and peace, or do they produce discouragement, despair, and anger? That idea could be terrifying to the point of sleepless nights! Who hasn't inadvertently said something that caused distress for someone else, even if that was never our intention? God help us!

Ah, but the good news is—God *does* help us! Not only does he forgive the sins and blunders of our past, but by his grace, he also empowers us to grow daily more and more into his likeness—to be like him.

Being like Christ begins with our mental choices.

Our "Christ-likeness" is measured by our relationships and how we treat the people around us. We choose to live by faith that the Holy Spirit will flow through us to touch the lives of others with his saving, redeeming, sustaining grace.

The Judgment is good news to those who are *in Christ.* "There is now no condemnation for those who are in Christ Jesus" (Romans 8:1).

Why is there no condemnation?

1. One, the sinless life record of Jesus is given to us as we accept his offer in exchange for our blemished record.

2. Second, when we are "in Christ," and Christ is "in us," we relate to others in positive, life-giving appreciation for who they are as individual human beings. We become more sensitive to the needs of other people, and we gradually learn how to respond to those needs in a Christ-like manner.

In his book *First Things First*,[34] Dr. Stephen Covey identifies four basic human needs: to live, to love, to learn, and to leave a legacy. By the single simple fact

---

[34] Covey, Stephen R., A. Roger Merrill, Rebecca R. Merrill; *First Things First: To Live, to Love, to Learn, to Leave a Legacy*; Simon & Schuster, New York NY, 1994.

of living in this world, every individual leaves a mark. We have no choice about that. But we do have a choice about the content of our legacy, aka the influence we leave behind. Will that influence be for better or for worse?

Our influence is the only thing we leave in this world. Everything else is transitory. A few generations pass and the memorable moments of individual lives fade into genealogy listings of vital statistics found only in dusty corners of obscure heritage libraries. Yet, the influence of our personal choices continues to live on through succeeding generations—sometimes with incredible power.

Look at this text from Hebrews 11:4 — "By faith Abel offered God a better sacrifice than Cain did. By faith he was commended as a righteous man, when God spoke well of his offerings. And by faith, he still speaks, even though he is dead."

And this from 2 Corinthians 9:2 — "I know your eagerness to help, and I have been boasting about it to the Macedonians, telling them that since last year you in Achaia were ready to give; and your enthusiasm has stirred most of them to action."

The Bible also gives examples of powerful influences for evil. For example, in his first letter to the Corinthians, Paul writes, "Your boasting is not good. Don't you know that a little yeast works through the whole batch of dough?" (1 Corinthians 5:6).

And again, a few chapters later, "Be careful . . . that the exercise of your freedom does not become a stumbling block to the weak" (1 Corinthians 8:9).

The Book of Genesis tells several multi-generational examples of negative influence.

In the account of Cain's descendants,[35] the story climaxes with Lamech, Cain's fifth-generation grandson. Lamech is the first individual who took two wives, then boasts to them about his ultra-conceited prowess as a murderer. The heritage from his ancestor Cain—who murdered his brother Able—has multiplied from generation to generation until it breaks out in this evil fruit of self-worshiping rebellion.

Another example comes following the story of Noah and the Flood.

The genealogical lines diverge again into lines of good and evil—specifically couched in the descendants of Shem, contrasted with that of his brothers Ham and Japheth. The "mighty warrior" Nimrod[36] was a grandson of Ham. Nimrod built the foundations of Babylon and other cultures which became the archenemies of Shem's descendants—the Semitic peoples—who were loyal to the worship of the Creator God. The influences of these ancients are still with us today! Just look at the never-ending conflicts in the Middle East!

But, before we get too mired in the muck of negativity, let's turn our eyes to some reasons for hope. People can—and do—change via the power of the living Christ!

In the chapter, "Wisdom for My Counsel," I quoted the Apostle Paul writing, "Jews demand

---

[35] Genesis 4:17-24.

[36] Genesis 10:8-11.

miraculous signs and Greeks look for wisdom, but we preach Christ crucified: a stumbling block to Jews and foolishness to Gentiles, but to those whom God has called, both Jews and Greeks, Christ the power of God and the wisdom of God" (1 Corinthians 1:22-25).

I can tell you from my own experience, God does change the trajectory of people—not just of individuals, but also of families through generation after generation.

You already know that severe alcoholism virtually destroyed my father's family of origin when his father— my grandfather Arthur Fenton—abandoned his wife and children to chase a bottle for the next several decades.[37] But the roots of this problem reached back at least one more generation to Arthur's father, and perhaps beyond.

The American Civil War created profound influences in the Fenton family line. During that terrible conflict Thomas W. Fenton—my great-grandfather— enlisted in the Iowa Infantry. Thomas was wounded during the Battle of Mark's Mills not far south of Little Rock, Arkansas. The entire Iowa 36th regiment was either killed, wounded, or captured and taken as prisoners-of-war to Camp Ford, Tyler, Texas.

Throughout the rest of his life, Thomas suffered great pain and difficulty from his old war wound. He died in 1901 at the age of sixty-eight.

At the end of the war and his subsequent release from the POW camp, Thomas returned north to Iowa. A few years later he married a young woman named Amelia

---

[37] See Chapter 5, "Strength for My Body," section on "Temperance."

Martin—his second wife. A few years later Amelia died giving birth to their fourth child. The baby was also lost.

Thomas and Amelia's third son, my grandfather Arthur, was two-and-a-half years old at the time of his mother's death.

The obvious emotional pain of losing two wives, the trauma of war—including those terrible months of POW confinement—and the heavy responsibility of raising three very young sons by himself created incredible stress in Thomas's life.

Following his wife's death, Thomas moved his family to a farm in Southwest Missouri near the town of Butler. His mother and an unmarried sister also made the move. They were needed to help care for the three motherless boys.

Unfortunately, it seems their home was a very unhappy place.

Aunt Lide (Eliza)—by all accounts—was a very mean person who constantly punished the growing boys, showing them no mercy for even the slightest missteps. Her unloving, hard discipline instilled a deep-seated anger/depression the boys carried with them through the rest of their life. One tragic result was the eventual murder-suicide by Edward, the oldest brother, who killed his wife in a drunken rage, and then turned the gun on himself.

When my grandfather Arthur abandoned his wife and children, Grandmother Hattie had no choice but to "farm her children out" to foster families willing to take them. Claude (age 11) went to live with a family named Leibecker somewhere in the Palouse Country of Eastern

Washington. By the time Claude was sixteen years old, he was on his own, working for a variety of ranchers around the region. At the outbreak of WWI, he enlisted in the US Marine Corps and spent two years stationed at Guantanamo Bay in Cuba.

As I mentioned in the previous chapter, my father absolutely refused to have anything to do with alcohol in any form, even in his years as a US Marine and as a ranch hand in the rough conditions on Eastern Washington wheat and cattle ranches.

His unbending stand against drinking and his consistent example was a major influence for my siblings and me. One of my daily prayers today for my entire extended family is that they can always stay free from this curse. The demon alcohol has not been good to us. I pray it will never again raise its ugly head.

Mark this down. YOUR influence can change the direction of another person's life and can continue generations into the future. By turning the power and extent of your influence over to God, you can be certain that it will only be used for good to accomplish his purposes. By your choices—and through the empowerment of God's grace—YOU can turn the tide of evil to leave a legacy of life, hope, healing, and encouragement for those who follow in your footsteps.

Now, I must bring all this to a close by telling you about three individuals whose combined influence powerfully changed the direction of my life. Because of these three, my walk with God came alive in ways I never knew before. Each served a separate purpose which merged seamlessly into God's master plan for me. Fused together by the Holy Spirit they formed the nucleus of my future life and ministry.

I have chosen to use their real names because I am eternally grateful for how their lives impacted mine. I share them here to honor what they did for me. Many others could be included, but here are three people who created a pivotal shift in my life's journey.

Doris Matson was the youth leader for our church family all through my growing-up years. She began teaching our cohort of church kids as pre-schoolers, then followed us as we graduated to Primary, then Juniors, and on into the teenage Youth class. Doris's long-term love inspired her devotion as our teacher and group mother, even after some of our group moved on to college, got married, or otherwise launched into adult living. She was always there for us—encouraging, supporting, sharing, inspiring, and wise.

Doris and her husband Merlin were just great people with a super-abundance of love for kids. Saturday nights often found us crowded into their home for popcorn, group games, and good times. We made a host of great memories.

Doris and Merlin's ministry made our youth group inspirational and fun. They helped us study the Bible, coached us as student leaders, and counseled as we organized our own events. They didn't just plan things for us. They opened the door and let us create our own vision of Christian living—all while giving invaluable guidance and focus. They never preached their values. They just lived them. Their counsel was pure gold.

The Matsons' influence in our youth group—and specifically for me—was truly profound. It was the first powerful stream of influence bringing me to my knees and to a true conversion to Christ.

The second was a high school friend I met by sheer coincidence.[38]

Bonita Etulain sat beside me in our high school Latin class. Seats were arranged in rigid alphabetical order. Her last name began with "E," mine with "F." Our desks sat adjacent to each other in the classroom's front row.

At the beginning of my sophomore year, I had absolutely no idea how much Bonita—one year older than me—would impact my life. Her personal influence that year opened the second spiritual stream merging into my experience. I didn't know it then, but God was right in the middle of this relationship working out his purpose for my future.

I normally should have been in our high school's Vocational Agriculture (VoAg) class instead of Latin. It was widely assumed—and pretty much expected—that high school boys from our farming community would enroll in VoAg and join Future Farmers of America (FFA). As a freshman (9th grade) I had followed the customary path. But when 10th grade rolled around I made a very strange decision.

From the early age of five, I had my sights set on becoming a veterinarian. In some sort of quirky thinking, I

---

[38] Is there really such a thing as pure coincidence? I don't think so! God is the great director of circumstances in life. He opens doors and orchestrates relationships to achieve his purposes.

decided that learning Latin would help me prepare for college training in veterinary medicine much more than VoAg or FFA.

Mr. Chase, my VoAg teacher certainly didn't see it that way, but he reluctantly signed my transfer request.

Academically, it was one of the biggest blunders of my entire formal education. I ended that year of Latin by totally failing the class! However, I have realized in later years that God's hand was guiding me, even then. In spite of the disastrous scholastic outcome, God placed me exactly where I needed to be for the new path he had ordained for me.

Our Latin teacher, Mr. Moga often provided quiet periods in class for us to study grammar, vocabulary, etc. No talking allowed! Stay focused! During one of the quiet study times, I sneaked a glance over to Bonita's desk to see what she was doing. I was surprised to see her memorizing Scripture verses on flashcards—not studying Latin!

Our public school included students from many faith backgrounds. I didn't know Bonita well at that point. I had no idea what church she and her family attended.

I quickly scribbled a note and slipped it onto her desk. "Why are you memorizing Bible texts?" I asked.

She wrote back, "It's for a Bible Bowl competition in YFC."

"YFC?" I responded. "What is that?" I guessed it must be the initials for her church's youth ministry.

"Youth for Christ," she answered. "You should come."

"Is that the name of your church youth group?"

"No, YFC is a Christian club for teens from any church. Everyone can be part of it. It doesn't matter what church you're from. We have a meeting this Friday after school at the Nazarene Church. Would you like to come?"

"Yes, I would," I quickly wrote my reply. "That sounds interesting."

The Nazarene Church building was right across the street from our high school. The next Friday I walked over to the church instead of getting on my bus to go home. Bonita and several other young people were already there.

"Hi, Loren! Welcome to YFC!" Everyone seemed excited to see me walk through the door.

I began attending the weekly meetings regularly and went with Bonita to monthly YFC rallies in Yakima—the "big city" of our county about 35 miles away. The next year I served as vice-president for our local club, and the following year—my senior year—I was elected president. During Christmas break in my junior year, I attended YFC's "Capitol Teen Convention" in Washington, D.C with approximately 12,000 other teenagers from all around the United States. One of the featured speakers was Dr. Billy Graham who addressed the gathering in person, along with many famous Christian sports stars, entertainers, and political personalities.

The focus of every YFC event—from our local club meetings to the regional rallies to the great national gatherings—was an invitation for every "unsaved" young person to accept Jesus Christ and God's free gift of eternal life. Not even training meetings for new club leaders or group recreational activities were exempt. Salvation by grace through faith permeated every thought, every plan, and every organizational body in YFC. Saving kids for eternity was—and is—YFC's continuing *raison d'être.*

My experience with Youth for Christ opened a door in my heart I had not fully understood before. My childhood church spoke often of grace and faith, but the heaviest emphasis was always on Obedience (with a capital "O"). God's Law was supreme. God's grace seemed secondary. But the light of God's love and grace shone brightly into my life through the ministry of YFC. It was through them I learned to walk with Jesus as my personal Savior and Lord.

This second stream of influence (salvation by grace through faith alone) blended perfectly with the first (positive social Christian fellowship).

The third stream arrived right on time—just when both of the others were in full force.

Evangelist Don Gray and his team came to our town (Sunnyside, Washington) with a big bubble tent in 1960 at the start of my sophomore year, and roughly the same time I began my involvement with Youth for Christ.

One October afternoon my friend Dale gave me a ride home after school. Dale drove north out of downtown Sunnyside on North 6th Street. As we neared the intersection of North 6th and what is now called Yakima Valley Highway, I suddenly saw this big air-supported tent pitched in a vacant lot on the east side of the street. It was huge!

"Oh, wow!" I shouted. "Look at that!"

Dale was busy driving and didn't see what I was so excited about.

"Turn around!" I said. "I want to see it better!"

Dale obliged and maneuvered to go back so we could get a better look. A large sign in front of the tent read, "BIBLE PROPHECY MEETINGS" giving the date for the opening night of an upcoming series of Bible lectures.

"That's really cool! I want to go to those meetings!"

Dale laughed at my enthusiasm, but I was serious. Opening night saw me—along with a couple hundred other people—crowded into the tent.

The interior was filled with rows and rows of chairs facing the speaker's wooden platform. A large booth housing movie and slide projectors stood at the back of the room. A giant screen mounted behind the platform displayed beautiful nature scenes while the people entered, then was used to show Bible quotations and illustrations for the sermon. A grand piano and an electric organ flanked the platform. Beautiful gospel music flooded the room. It was awesome! I was "in heaven."

The organizers of the meetings had an attendance incentive feature in place. A person attending 25 of the 30 scheduled meetings could receive a brand-new Bible as a thank-you gift. I was determined to get my Bible. I didn't have one of my own and this was a good opportunity. It was a happy moment when I got my 25th hole punched in the record card and I took possession of my very own King James Bible.

I learned a lot attending Evangelist Gray's lectures. He had a nightly travelogue with home movies and color slides he had personally taken during a recent trip around the world. He told fascinating stories linking ancient history and current events relevant to the nations and cultures he visited, and how they fit into the biblical prophecies of end times.

On one evening toward the end of the series, Evangelist Gray showed a beautiful picture of Christ with hands outstretched in invitation. The appeal stirred my heart, and I went forward together with several other people. We were ushered to a small area at the back of the platform where several chairs had been placed to accommodate the seekers. After we were seated the evangelist spoke to us about our personal walk with God.

"I have two Bible texts to share with you," he began. "I encourage you to memorize these texts and underline them in your Bible."

He then had us open our Bibles.

"The first text is 1 John 1:7," he said. "Here it is: *If we walk in the light, as he is in the light, we have fellowship one with another, and the blood of Jesus Christ his Son cleanseth us from all sin.*

"The second text is very similar, and it is only two verses later in the same chapter. It is 1 John 1:9: *If we confess our sins, he is faithful and just to forgive us our sins, and to cleanse us from all unrighteousness.*[39]"

---

[39] Both texts quoted here are from the KJV.

117

I never forgot that moment or those two texts. They have bolstered my faith time and time again through all the many years since.

Several months passed after I responded to that call. It was nearly a year later in the early weeks of the next school year—Fall of 1961—when I walked out under the stars and opened my heart fully to God.[40]

I have only recently realized the role each of these powerful streams of witness played in bringing me to that point of submission and confession.

- The ministry of Doris and Merlin Matson—combined with a vibrant youth fellowship in my home church—provided an essential positive social environment to anchor my nascent personal walk with God.

- The faithful Christian witness of Bonita Etulain who drew me into involvement with Youth for Christ where my heart was opened more fully to the gospel of salvation by grace through faith.

- The Spirit-filled, Bible-based teaching of Evangelist Don Gray whose presence brought timely instruction in Bible truths, a Christian understanding of history, and a sharpened awareness of last-day events as foretold by the ancient prophetic words of Scripture.

---

[40] Read my conversion story in the Introduction at the beginning of this book.

The memory of these dear friends continues to energize my faith and empower my devotion to Christ even now, nearly sixty years hence. And thus, I pray every day that my own influence will rightly represent the King I serve, touching the lives of others with life, hope, healing, and encouragement. I share these thoughts, praying that you also will join me in this walk of faith.

It is a joyful journey. Let's go!

Chapter Eight
Building the Firewall

Establishing The Seven Essential Daily Prayers as a Daily Experience[41]

How can a young man keep his way pure? By living according to your word. I seek you with all my heart; do not let me stray from your commands. I have hidden your word in my heart that I might not sin against you (Psalm 119:9-11).

We have covered a lot of ground in these seven chapters: Purity, Righteousness, Integrity, Joy, Strength, Wisdom, and Influence. I pray the thoughts I have shared on these pages may be an encouragement and a blessing to you.

In my spiritual journey, I have discovered how important it is to have a special time every morning for

---

[41] The bulk of this chapter is taken from a book I wrote and published in 1977. *Thirteen Weeks to Riches: Which Could Be Glory* was my first attempt at writing and self-publishing a book. The last chapter in *Thirteen Weeks* was titled "Daily Growth." I have adapted and updated some of the content here. I have a limited number of the original *Thirteen Weeks* books available at https://lorenfentonauthor.com/store

prayer, Bible reading, and personal growth. Most recently, as my understanding of the Seven Essential Daily Prayers developed they became a top-priority item in my daily list of concerns for family, friends, loved ones, other needs.

> **Key Concept:**
> *A habit of personal devotions at the beginning of every day will revolutionize your walk with God.*

Through the years my devotional experience has grown deeper and wider with new understandings and practices. Here is a brief account of one of those pivotal moments in my walk with God—a moment that set me on a path of discovering rich, meaningful principles of prayer. Perhaps it will encourage you as it did me.

Many years ago, I was at a special conference on the importance and practice of prayer. The speaker was a retired minister about seventy years old. He had more spark and energy than I've seen in many men much younger! He related to everything and everybody with a divine enthusiasm for life.

Pastor Glenn Coon told of his experience when he left home to attend college. His father, a godly man, took him to the railroad station. Before they parted, they prayed together, then his father gave him this advice: *Spend at least one hour every day with the Lord—no matter what.*

When Glenn arrived at the college, he got a job milking cows on the college farm. He had to leave for work at 4:00 a.m. A busy school program kept him quite busy with classes and study until late at night, so to get his "hour with the Lord" he had to get up at 3:00 a.m. He did this faithfully every morning all during his college years.

At the prayer conference Pastor Coon told us, "I have continued the habit of spending an hour with God every morning. Not always at 3:00 a.m., but every morning before anything else has a chance to interrupt. My time with the Lord has always had the highest priority. It is this habit—more than anything else—that has energized my life and given me the strength I need every day."

When I heard Pastor Coon's testimony I was inspired to follow his example. Back home following the conference, I set my alarm clock for a half-hour earlier than my normal wake-up time. When it rang the next morning I headed downstairs to my study. I was excited to begin this new adventure in prayer. I closed and locked the door behind me and sat down at my desk.

Suddenly, confronted by an empty sixty-minute block of time, I realized I had no idea how I could ever spend a full hour in communion with God.

"Lord," I prayed, "teach me what I should do now. I confess, I don't know what to do or say."

An idea occurred to me. I thought, *If prayer is a two-way conversation with God, part of prayer is Bible study and good Christian reading material, letting God speak to me through inspired literature. I can divide the hour into three 20-minute segments: the first twenty minutes for reading; the second period for Bible study; the third for sharing my thoughts with him.*

Behind me on the wall was a whole library of books and other miscellaneous reading materials. I picked out a book I'd been wanting to read for some time, opened it, and began my journey. At the end of the allotted time, I put in a page marker and set the book in a special place on my desk, then turned my attention to the Bible.

How to study it?

I had read the Bible through from cover to cover a couple of times already. I didn't want to do the same thing over again. I wanted variety.

I couldn't think of any special way to study the Bible that morning, so I decided just to read the New Testament in a modern translation. That would be a change. I picked up Today's English Version (TEV).

At the end of twenty minutes, I could hardly stop reading. I forced myself to put in a marker and place it next to the first book on my desk.

Now came the real trial. How could I spend an entire twenty minutes on my knees? Twenty minutes seemed as formidable as a fortress! Previously, I had never been able to spend even five minutes in prayer without getting bored. But now, here I was. The time had come. I pushed my chair back and knelt before my desk.

"Lord," I prayed again, "I don't know how to pray like this. Help me know—and teach me to pray the way you want me to."

I didn't hear any trumpets or audible sounds, but once again I sensed in my spirit the same voice speaking as when I gave my heart to Jesus many years before. I recognized him immediately. The Holy Spirit directed my thoughts to the story of Jesus teaching his disciples about prayer.

Still on my knees, I got my Bible and turned to the Lord's Prayer.[42] As I studied this model prayer, I saw it was divided into three major parts: praise; requests; and praise.

So, that's my trouble! I thought. *All I've ever done in prayer is make requests. What I need to do is begin and end my prayer with praise!*

I closed my eyes again and started to praise the Lord.

But, the thought crossed my mind, *what should I praise him for? Isn't praise supposed to be thanksgiving for blessings received?*

Then it came to my mind that our praise of God—our worship of him—doesn't depend on whether he has done anything for us or not. We should worship him and praise him simply because he is *worthy* of worship. He is worthy of praise!

I couldn't contain my joy with this discovery! I raised my hands, palms opened and arms wide in adoration and worship of the Great Creator/Redeemer. An overpowering sense of love and awe swept over me. I didn't have to contribute anything—just to be there in his presence and worship him was enough.

After a few moments, I shared with the Lord some personal needs and concerns. I spoke them aloud and thanked him in advance for answering my prayers

[42] Matthew 6:9-13.

according to his wisdom and love. I ended my devotional time with another session of praise and worship.

I looked at my watch. My twenty minutes were just finishing. I hadn't been bored at all! It was a thrilling experience—one I wouldn't trade for anything.

But, here's another truth I have learned in my spiritual journey.

If you are looking for a wonderful experience with God, you must not make *the experience* primary. You must make *God himself* the object of your adoration and praise. We must not worship the experience we seek. Instead, we must worship God alone. He alone is worthy.

I've chosen to finish this book with the words of an old Christian hymn I first heard as a child in church. They seem to be an appropriate benediction for ending our exploration of the *Seven Essential Daily Prayers*.

Take My Life and Let it Be (Francis Ridley Havergal, 1874)

> (Verse 1)
> Take my life and let it be
> Consecrated, Lord, to Thee;
> Take my hands and let them move
> At the impulse of Thy love,
> At the impulse of Thy love.
>
> (Verse 2)
> Take my feet and let them be
> Swift and beautiful for Thee;
> Take my voice, and let me sing

Always, only, for my King,
Always, only, for my King.

(Verse 3)
Take my lips and let them be
Filled with messages from Thee;
Take my silver and my gold,
Not a mite would I withhold,
Not a mite would I withhold.

(Verse 4)
Take my will and make it Thine;
It shall be no longer mine;
Take my heart it is Thine own,
It shall be Thy royal throne,
It shall be Thy royal throne.

(Verse 5)
Take my love; my Lord, I pour
At Thy feet its treasure store;
Take my-self, and I will be,
Ever, only, all for Thee,
Ever, only, all for Thee

About the Author

Loren L. Fenton, D.Min., was born and raised in Washington State, USA. He is a graduate of Sunnyside, Washington High School (1963), Walla Walla University (1967), and Andrews University (1971 and 1998). Over the course of his lifetime, he has been a pastor, evangelist, missionary, husband, father, and grandfather.

Loren and his wife Ruth have two children and five grandchildren. They have lived in Washington, Oregon, California, Michigan, West Virginia, Ohio, and Taiwan. They have also toured in China, The Philippines, Israel, Egypt, and many States in the USA. They currently enjoy retirement living in College Place, Washington, where they keep active writing blogs and books, as well as participating in various ministries conducted by their local church.

You can visit Loren's website at
https://LorenFentonAuthor.com

Additional Resources
from
GoodlifeNews! Productions

1) Personal and Group STUDY GUIDES for the *Seven Essential Daily Prayers* for men's and women's ministries, prayer meetings, etc. Contact *loren@lorenfentonauthor.com* for availability.

2) BOOKS by Loren L. Fenton

   a) *"Whoa," I Yelled, "Whoa!": A Collection of Stories from My Childhood and Youth.*

   b) *Whimsi and The Big Election.* (Illustrated by Kimberly Holback)

   c) *Thirteen Weeks to Riches: Which Could be Glory*

3) VIDEO

   a) *Seven Essential Daily Prayers.* A self-paced video course with seven individual lessons. Includes short review quizzes and downloadable lesson outlines. Online: *https://www.goodlifenews-academy.thinkific.com*

4) OTHER WEBSITES

   a) *https://goodlifenews.co*

   b) *www.amazon.com/author/lorenfenton*